HOW

SUCCESSFUL

PEOPLE THINK

Also by John C. Maxwell:

ETHICS 101

THE 15 INVALUABLE LAWS OF
GROWTH

THE 5 LEVELS OF LEADERSHIP

HOW SUCCESSFUL PEOPLE LEAD

MAKE TODAY COUNT

RUNNING WITH THE GIANTS

SOMETIMES YOU WIN—
SOMETIMES YOU LEARN

THERE'S NO SUCH THING AS
"BUSINESS" ETHICS

THINKING FOR A CHANGE

TODAY MATTERS

HOW
SUCCESSFUL
PEOPLE THINK

CHANGE YOUR THINKING,
CHANGE YOUR LIFE

JOHN C. MAXWELL

CENTER STREET®

New York   Boston   Nashville

Scriptures noted NIV are taken from the HOLY BIBLE: NEW INTERNATIONAL VERSION®. Copyright © 1973, 1978, 1984 by International Bible Society. Used by permission of Zondervan Publishing House. All rights reserved. Scriptures noted NRSV are taken from the NEW REVISED STANDARD VERSION of the Bible. Copyright © 1989 by the Division of Christian Education of the National Council of The Churches of Christ in the U.S.A. All rights reserved.

The author is represented by Yates & Yates, LLP, Literary Agency, Orange, California.

Center Street
Hachette Book Group
1290 Avenue of the Americas
New York, NY 10104
www.centerstreet.com

Center Street is a division of Hachette Book Group, Inc. The Center Street name and logo are trademarks of Hachette Book Group, Inc.

The Hachette Speakers Bureau provides a wide range of authors for speaking events. To find out more, go to www.hachettespeakersbureau.com or call (866) 376-6591.

The publisher is not responsible for websites (or their content) that are not owned by the publisher.

Printed in the United States of America
Originally published as *Thinking for a Change* by Center Street, 2003
First Center Street Edition: June 2009
30 29 28 27 26 25 24 23 22

Library of Congress Cataloging-in-Publication Data
Maxwell, John C.
How successful people think : change your thinking, change your life / John C. Maxwell. — 1st ed.
    p. cm.
ISBN 978-1-59995-168-3
1. Success — Psychological aspects. 2. Thought and thinking. I. Title.
BF637.S8M3417 2009
158.1 — dc22

2008029844

Interior design by Charles Sutherland

ACKNOWLEDGMENTS

I'd like to say thank you to

Margaret Maxwell,
who shares her thinking with me daily

Charlie Wetzel,
who does my writing

Stephanie Wetzel,
who proofs and edits the manuscript, and

Linda Eggers,
who runs my life

CONTENTS

INTRODUCTION

Good thinkers are always in demand. A person who knows *how* may always have a job, but the person who knows *why* will always be his boss. Good thinkers solve problems, they never lack ideas that can build an organization, and they always have hope for a better future. Good thinkers rarely find themselves at the mercy of ruthless people who would take advantage of them or try to deceive them, people like Nazi dictator Adolf Hitler, who once boasted, "What luck for rulers that men do not think." Those who develop the process of good thinking can rule themselves—even while under an oppressive ruler or in other difficult circumstances. In short, good thinkers are successful.

I've studied successful people for forty years, and though the diversity you find among them is astounding, I've found that they are all alike in one way: how they think! That is the one thing that separates successful people from unsuccessful ones. And here's the good news. How successful people think can be learned. If you change your thinking, you can change your life!

WHY YOU SHOULD CHANGE YOUR THINKING

It's hard to overstate the value of changing your thinking. Good thinking can do many things for you: generate revenue, solve problems, and create opportunities. It can take you to a whole new level—personally and professionally. It really can change your life.

Consider some things you need to know about changing your thinking:

1. Changed Thinking Is Not Automatic

Sadly, a change in thinking doesn't happen on its own. Good ideas rarely go out and find someone. If you want to find a good idea, you must search for it. If you want to become a better thinker, you need to work at it—and once you begin to become a better thinker, the good ideas keep coming. In fact, the amount of good thinking you can do at any time depends primarily on the amount of good thinking you are already doing.

2. Changed Thinking Is Difficult

When you hear someone say, "Now this is just off the top of my head," expect dandruff. The only people who believe thinking is easy are those who don't habitually engage in it. Nobel Prize-winning physicist Albert Einstein, one of the best thinkers who ever lived, asserted, "Thinking is hard work; that's why so few do it." Because thinking is so difficult, you want to use anything you can to help you improve the process.

3. Changed Thinking Is Worth the Investment

Author Napoleon Hill observed, "More gold has been mined from the thoughts of man than has ever been taken from the earth." When you take the time to learn how to change your thinking and become a better thinker, you are investing in yourself. Gold mines tap out. Stock markets crash. Real estate investments can go sour. But a human mind with the ability to think well is like a diamond mine that never runs out. It's priceless.

HOW TO BECOME A BETTER THINKER

Do you want to master the process of good thinking? Do you want to be a better thinker tomorrow than you are today? Then you need to engage in an ongoing process that improves your thinking. I recommend you do the following:

1. Expose Yourself to Good Input

Good thinkers always prime the pump of ideas. They always look for things to get the thinking process started, because what you put in always impacts what comes out.

Read books, review trade magazines, listen to tapes, and spend time with good thinkers. And when something intrigues you—whether it's someone else's idea or the seed of an idea that you've come up with yourself—keep it in front of you. Put it in writing and keep it somewhere in your favorite thinking place to stimulate your thinking.

2. Expose Yourself to Good Thinkers

Spend time with the right people. As I worked on this section and bounced my ideas off of some key people (so that my thoughts would be stretched), I realized something about myself. All of the people in my life whom I consider to be close friends or colleagues are thinkers. Now, I love all people. I try to be kind to everyone I meet, and I desire to add value to as many people as I can through conferences, books, audio lessons, etc. But the people I seek out and choose to spend time with all challenge me with their thinking and their actions. They are constantly trying to grow and learn. That's true of my wife, Margaret, my close friends, and the executives who run my companies. Every one of them is a good thinker!

The writer of Proverbs observed that sharp people sharpen one another, just as iron sharpens iron. If you want to be a sharp thinker, be around sharp people.

3. Choose to Think Good Thoughts

To become a good thinker, you must become intentional about the thinking process. Regularly put yourself in the right place to think, shape, stretch, and land your thoughts. Make it a priority. Remember, thinking is a discipline.

Recently I had breakfast with Dan Cathy, the president

of Chick-fil-A, a fast food chain headquartered in the Atlanta area. I told him that I was working on this book and I asked him if he made thinking time a high priority. Not only did he say yes, but he told me about what he calls his "thinking schedule." It helps him to fight the hectic pace of life that discourages intentional thinking. Dan says he sets aside time just to think for half a day every two weeks, for one whole day every month, and for two or three full days every year. Dan explains, "This helps me 'keep the main thing, the main thing,' since I am so easily distracted."

You may want to do something similar, or you can develop a schedule and method of your own. No matter what you choose to do, go to your thinking place, take paper and pen, and make sure you capture your ideas in writing.

4. Act on Your Good Thoughts

Ideas have a short shelf life. You must act on them before the expiration date. World War I flying ace Eddie Rickenbacker said it all when he remarked, "I can give you a six-word formula for success: Think things through—then follow through."

5. Allow Your Emotions to Create Another Good Thought

To start the thinking process, you cannot rely on your feelings. In *Failing Forward*, I wrote that you can act your way into feeling long before you can feel your way into action. If you wait until you feel like doing something, you will likely never accomplish it. The same is true for thinking. You cannot wait until you *feel* like thinking to do it.

However, I've found that once you engage in the process of good thinking, you can use your emotions to feed the process and create mental momentum.

Try it for yourself. After you go through the disciplined process of thinking and enjoy some success, allow yourself to savor the moment and try riding the mental energy of that success. If you're like me, it's likely to spur additional thoughts and productive ideas.

6. Repeat the Process

One good thought does not make a good life. The people who have one good thought and try to ride it for an entire career often end up unhappy or destitute. They are the one-hit wonders, the one-book authors, the one-message speakers, the one-time inventors who spend their life struggling to protect or promote their single idea. Success comes to those who have an entire mountain of gold that they continually mine, not those who find one nugget and try to live on it for fifty years. To become someone who can mine a lot of gold, you need to keep repeating the process of good thinking.

PUTTING YOURSELF IN THE RIGHT PLACE TO THINK

Becoming a good thinker isn't overly complicated. It's a discipline. If you do the six things I have outlined above, you will set yourself up for a lifestyle of better thinking. But what do you do to come up with specific ideas on a day-to-day basis?

I want to teach you the process that I've used to discover and develop good thoughts. It's certainly not the only one that works, but it has worked well for me.

1. Find a Place to Think Your Thoughts

If you go to your designated place to think expecting to generate good thoughts, then eventually you will come up with some. Where is the best place to think? Everybody's different. Some people think best in the shower. Others, like my friend Dick Biggs, like to go to a park. For me, the best places to think are in my car, on planes, and in the spa. Ideas come to me in other places as well, such as when I'm in bed. (I keep a special lighted writing pad on my night-stand for such times.) I believe I often get thoughts because I make it a habit to frequently go to my thinking places. If you want to consistently generate ideas, you need to do the same thing. Find a place where you can think, and plan to capture your thoughts on paper so that you don't lose them. When I found a place to think my thoughts, my thoughts found a place in me.

2. Find a Place to Shape Your Thoughts

Rarely do ideas come fully formed and completely worked out. Most of the time, they need to be shaped until they have substance. As my friend Dan Reiland says, they have to "stand the test of clarity and questioning." During the shaping time, you want to hold an idea up to strong scrutiny. Many times a thought that seemed outstanding late at night looks pretty silly in the light of day. Ask questions about your ideas. Fine tune them. One of the best ways to do that is to put your thoughts in writing. Professor, college president, and U.S. senator S. I. Hayakawa wrote, "Learning to write is learning to think. You don't know anything clearly unless you can state it in writing."

As you shape your thoughts, you find out whether an idea has potential. You learn what you have. You also learn some things about yourself. The shaping time thrills me because it embodies:

- **Humor:** The thoughts that don't work often provide comic relief.
- **Humility:** The moments when I connect with God awe me.
- **Excitement:** I love to play out an idea mentally. (I call it "futuring" it.)
- **Creativity:** In these moments I am unhampered by reality.
- **Fulfillment:** God made me for this process; it uses my greatest gifts and gives me joy.
- **Honesty:** As I turn over an idea in my mind, I discover my true motives.
- **Passion:** When you shape a thought, you find out what you believe and what really counts.
- **Change:** Most of the changes I have made in my life resulted from thorough thinking on a subject.

You can shape your thoughts almost anywhere. Just find a place that works for you, where you will be able to write things down, focus your attention without interruptions, and ask questions about your ideas.

3. Find a Place to Stretch Your Thoughts

If you come upon great thoughts and spend time mentally shaping them, don't think you're done and can stop there. If you do, you will miss some of the most valuable aspects of the thinking process. You miss bringing others in and expanding ideas to their greatest potential.

Earlier in my life, I have to admit, I was often guilty of this error. I wanted to take an idea from seed thought to solution before sharing it with anyone, even the people it would most impact. I did this both at work and at home. But over the years, I have learned that you can go much farther with a team than you can go alone.

I've found a kind of formula that can help you stretch your thoughts. It says,

The Right **Thought** plus the Right **People**

in the Right **Environment** at the Right **Time**

for the Right **Reason** = the **Right Result**

This combination is hard to beat. Like every person, every thought has the potential to become something great. When you find a place to stretch your thoughts, you find that potential.

4. Find a Place to Land Your Thoughts

Author C. D. Jackson observes that "great ideas need landing gear as well as wings." Any idea that remains only an idea doesn't make a great impact. The real power of an idea comes when it goes from abstraction to application. Think about Einstein's theory of relativity. When he published his theories in 1905 and 1916, they were merely profound ideas. Their real power came with the development of the nuclear reactor in 1942 and the nuclear bomb in 1945. When scientists developed and implemented Einstein's ideas, the whole world changed.

Likewise, if you want your thoughts to make an impact, you need to land them with others so that they can someday be implemented. As you plan for the application phase of the thinking process, land your ideas first with . . .

- **Yourself:** Landing an idea with yourself will give you integrity. People will buy into an idea only after they buy into the leader who communicates it. Before teaching any lesson, I ask myself three questions: "Do I believe it? Do I live it? Do I believe others should live it?" If I can't answer yes to all three questions, then I haven't landed it.
- **Key Players:** Let's face it, no idea will fly if the influencers don't embrace it. After all, they are the people who carry thoughts from idea to implementation.
- **Those Most Affected:** Landing thoughts with the people on the firing line will give you great insight. Those closest to changes that occur as a result of a

new idea can give you a "reality read." And that's important, because sometimes even when you've diligently completed the process of creating a thought, shaping it, and stretching it with other good thinkers, you can still miss the mark.

5. Find a Place to Fly Your Thoughts

French philosopher Henri-Louis Bergson, who won the Nobel Prize in literature in 1927, asserted that a person should "think like a man of action—act like a man of thought." What good is thinking if it has no application in real life? Thinking divorced from actions cannot be productive. Learning how to master the process of thinking well leads you to productive thinking. If you can develop the discipline of good thinking and turn it into a lifetime habit, then you will be successful and productive all of your life. Once you've created, shaped, stretched, and landed your thoughts, then flying them can be fun and easy.

PORTRAIT OF A GOOD THINKER

You often hear someone say that a colleague or friend is a "good thinker," but that phrase means something different to everyone. To one person it may mean having a high IQ, while to another it could mean knowing a bunch of trivia or being able to figure out whodunit when reading a mystery novel. I believe that good thinking isn't just one thing. It consists of several specific thinking skills. Becoming a good thinker means developing those skills to the best of your ability.

It doesn't matter whether you were born rich or poor. It doesn't matter if you have a third grade education or possess a Ph.D. It doesn't matter if you suffer from multiple disabilities or you're the picture of health. No matter what your circumstances, you can learn to be a good thinker. All you must do is be willing to engage in the process every day.

In *Built to Last*, Jim Collins and Jerry Porras describe what it means to be a visionary company, the kind of company that epitomizes the pinnacle of American business. They describe those companies this way:[1]

A visionary company is like a great work of art. Think of Michelangelo's scenes from Genesis on the ceiling of the Sistine Chapel or his statue of David. Think of a great and enduring novel like *Huckleberry Finn* or *Crime and Punishment*. Think of Beethoven's Ninth Symphony or Shakespeare's *Henry V*. Think of a beautifully designed building, like the masterpieces of Frank Lloyd Wright or Ludwig Mies van der Rohe. You can't point to any one single item that makes the whole thing work; it's the entire work—all the pieces working together to create an overall effect—that leads to enduring greatness.

Good thinking is similar. You need all the thinking "pieces" to become the kind of person who can achieve great things. Those pieces include the following eleven skills:

- Seeing the Wisdom of Big-Picture Thinking
- Unleashing the Potential of Focused Thinking
- Discovering the Joy of Creative Thinking
- Recognizing the Importance of Realistic Thinking
- Releasing the Power of Strategic Thinking
- Feeling the Energy of Possibility Thinking
- Embracing the Lessons of Reflective Thinking
- Questioning the Acceptance of Popular Thinking
- Encouraging the Participation of Shared Thinking
- Experiencing the Satisfaction of Unselfish Thinking
- Enjoying the Return of Bottom-Line Thinking

As you read the chapters dedicated to each kind of thinking, you will discover that they do not try to tell you *what* to think; they attempt to teach you *how* to think. As you become acquainted with each skill, you will find that some you do well, others you don't. Learn to develop each of those kinds of thinking, and you will become a better thinker. Master all that you can—including the process of shared thinking which helps you compensate for your weak areas—and your life will change.

HOW
SUCCESSFUL
PEOPLE THINK

1

Cultivate Big-Picture Thinking

"Where success is concerned, people are not measured in inches, or pounds, or college degrees, or family background; they are measured by the size of their thinking."
—DAVID SCHWARTZ

Big-picture thinking can benefit any person in any profession. When somebody like Jack Welch tells a GE employee that the ongoing relationship with the customer is more important than the sale of an individual product, he's reminding them of the big picture. When two parents are fed up with potty training, poor grades, or fender-benders, and one reminds the other that the current difficult time is only a temporary season, then they benefit from thinking big picture. Real estate developer Donald Trump quipped, "You have to think anyway, so why not think big?" Big-picture thinking brings wholeness and maturity to a person's thinking. It brings perspective. It's like making the frame of a picture bigger, in the process expanding not only what you can see, but what you are able to do.

Spend time with big-picture thinkers, and you will find that they:

Learn Continually

Big-picture thinkers are never satisfied with what they already know. They are always visiting new places, reading new books, meeting new people, learning new skills. And because of that practice, they often are able to connect the unconnected. They are lifelong learners.

To help me maintain a learner's attitude, I spend a few moments every morning thinking about my learning opportunities for the day. As I review my calendar and to-do list—knowing whom I will meet that day, what I will read, which meetings I will attend—I note where I am most likely to learn something. Then I mentally cue myself to look attentively for something that will improve me in that situation. If you desire to keep learning, I want to encourage you to examine your day and look for opportunities to learn.

Listen Intentionally

An excellent way to broaden your experience is to listen to someone who has expertise in an area where you don't. I search for such opportunities. One year I spoke to about 900 coaches and scouts at the Senior Bowl, where graduating football players participate in their last college game. I had the opportunity, along with my son-in-law, Steve Miller, to have dinner with NFL head coaches Dave

Wannstedt and Butch Davis. It's not often that you get such an opportunity, so I asked them questions about teamwork and spent a lot of time listening to them. At the end of the evening, as Steve and I were walking to our car, he said to me, "John, I bet you asked those coaches a hundred questions tonight."

"If I'm going to learn and grow," I replied, "I must know what questions to ask and know how to apply the answers to my life. Listening has taught me a lot more than talking."

When you meet with people, it's good to have an agenda so that you can learn. It's a great way to partner with people who can do things you can't. Big-picture thinkers recognize that they don't know lots of things. They frequently ask penetrating questions to enlarge their understanding and thinking. If you want to become a better big-picture thinker, then become a good listener.

Look Expansively

Writer Henry David Thoreau wrote, "Many an object is not seen, though it falls within the range of our visual ray, because it does not come within the range of our intellectual ray." Human beings habitually see their own world first. For example, when people arrive at a leadership conference put on by my company, they want to know where they're going to park, whether they will be able to get a good (and comfortable) seat, whether the speaker will be "on," and if the breaks will be spaced right. When I arrive to speak at the same conference, I want to know that the lighting is good, the sound equipment is operating effectively, whether the speaker's platform will be close enough to the people, etc. Who you are determines what you see—and how you think.

Big-picture thinkers realize there is a world out there besides their own, and they make an effort to get outside of themselves and see other people's worlds through their eyes. It's hard to see the picture while inside the frame. To see how others see, you must first find out how they think. Becoming a good listener certainly helps with that. So does getting over your personal agenda and trying to take the other person's perspective.

Live Completely

French essayist Michel Eyquem de Montaigne wrote, "The value of life lies not in the length of days, but in the use we make of them; a man may live long yet live very little." The truth is that you can spend your life any way you want, but you can spend it only once. Becoming a big-picture thinker can help you to live with wholeness, to live a very fulfilling life. People who see the big picture expand their experience because they expand their world. As a result, they accomplish more than narrow-minded people. And they experience fewer unwanted surprises, too, because they are more likely to see the many components involved in any given situation: issues, people, relationships, timing, and values. They are also, therefore, usually more tolerant of other people and their thinking.

WHY YOU SHOULD RECEIVE THE WISDOM OF BIG-PICTURE THINKING

Intuitively, you probably recognize big-picture thinking as beneficial. Few people want to be closed-minded. No one sets out to be that way. But just in case you're not completely convinced, consider several specific reasons why you should make the effort to become a better big-picture thinker:

1. Big-Picture Thinking Allows You to Lead

You can find many big-picture thinkers who aren't leaders, but you will find few leaders who are not big-picture thinkers. Leaders must be able to do many important things for their people:

- **See the vision before their people do.** They also see more of it. This allows them to . . .
- **Size up situations, taking into account many variables.** Leaders who see the big picture discern possibilities as well as problems to form a foundation to build the vision. Once leaders have done that, they can . . .
- **Sketch a picture of where the team is going,** including any potential challenges or obstacles. The goal of leaders shouldn't be merely to make their people feel good, but to help them be good and accomplish the dream. The vision, shown accurately, will allow leaders to . . .
- **Show how the future connects with the past to**

make the journey more meaningful. When leaders recognize this need for connection and bridge it, then they can . . .

- **Seize the moment when the timing is right.** In leadership, when to move is as important as what you do. As Winston Churchill said, "There comes a special moment in everyone's life, a moment for which that person was born. . . . When he seizes it . . . it is his finest hour."

Whether building roads, planning a trip, or moving in leadership, big-picture thinking allows you to enjoy more success. People who are constantly looking at the whole picture have the best chance of succeeding in any endeavor.

2. Big-Picture Thinking Keeps You on Target

Thomas Fuller, chaplain to Charles II of England, observed, "He that is everywhere is nowhere." To get things done, you need focus. However, to get the right things done, you also need to consider the big picture. Only by putting your daily activities in the context of the big picture will you be able to stay on target. As Alvin Toffler says, "You've got to think about 'big things' while you're doing small things, so that all the small things go in the right direction."

3. Big-Picture Thinking Allows You to See What Others See

One of the most important skills you can develop in

human relations is the ability to see things from the other person's point of view. It's one of the keys to working with clients, satisfying customers, maintaining a marriage, rearing children, helping those who are less fortunate, etc. All human interactions are enhanced by the ability to put yourself in another person's shoes. How? Look beyond yourself, your own interests, and your own world. When you work to consider an issue from every possible angle, examine it in the light of another's history, discover the interests and concerns of others, and try to set aside your own agenda, you begin to see what others see. And that is a powerful thing.

4. Big-Picture Thinking Promotes Teamwork

If you participate in any kind of team activity, then you know how important it is that team members see the whole picture, not just their own part. Anytime a person doesn't know how his work fits with that of his teammates, then the whole team is in trouble. The better the grasp team members have of the big picture, the greater their potential to work together as a team.

5. Big-Picture Thinking Keeps You from Being Caught Up in the Mundane

Let's face it: some aspects of everyday life are absolutely necessary but thoroughly uninteresting. Big-picture thinkers don't let the grind get to them, because they don't lose sight of the all-important overview. They know that the person who forgets the ultimate is a slave to the immediate.

6. Big-Picture Thinking Helps You to Chart Uncharted Territory

Have you ever heard the expression, "We'll cross that bridge when we come to it"? That phrase undoubtedly was coined by someone who had trouble seeing the big picture. The world was built by people who "crossed bridges" in their minds long before anyone else did. The only way to break new ground or move into uncharted territory is to look beyond the immediate and see the big picture.

HOW TO ACQUIRE THE WISDOM OF BIG-PICTURE THINKING

If you desire to seize new opportunities and open new horizons, then you need to add big-picture thinking to your abilities. To become a good thinker better able to see the big picture, keep in mind the following suggestions:

1. Don't Strive for Certainty

Big-picture thinkers are comfortable with ambiguity. They don't try to force every observation or piece of data into pre-formulated mental cubby holes. They think broadly and can juggle many seemingly contradictory thoughts in their minds. If you want to cultivate the ability to think big picture, then you must get used to embracing and dealing with complex and diverse ideas.

2. Learn from Every Experience

Big-picture thinkers broaden their outlook by striving to learn from every experience. They don't rest on their successes, they learn from them. More importantly, they learn from their failures. They can do that because they remain teachable.

Varied experiences—both positive and negative—help you see the big picture. The greater the variety of experience and success, the more potential to learn you have. If you desire to be a big-picture thinker, then get out there and try a lot of things, take a lot of chances, and take time to learn after every victory or defeat.

3. Gain Insight from a Variety of People

Big-picture thinkers learn from their experiences. But they also learn from experiences they don't have. That is, they learn by receiving insight from others—from customers, employees, colleagues, and leaders.

If you desire to broaden your thinking and see more of the big picture, then seek out counselors to help you. But be wise in whom you ask for advice. Gaining insight from a variety of people doesn't mean stopping anyone and everyone in hallways and grocery store lines and asking what they think about a given subject. Be selective. Talk to people who know and care about you, who know their field, and who bring experience deeper and broader than your own.

4. Give Yourself Permission to Expand Your World

If you want to be a big-picture thinker, you will have to go against the flow of the world. Society wants to keep people in boxes. Most people are married mentally to the status quo. They want what was, not what can be. They seek safety and simple answers. To think big-picture, you need to give yourself permission to go a different way, to break new ground, to find new worlds to conquer. And when your world does get bigger, you need to celebrate. Never forget there is more out there in the world than what you've experienced.

Keep learning, keep growing, and keep looking at the big picture! If you desire to be a good thinker, that's what you need to do.

Thinking Question

Am I thinking beyond myself and my world so that I process ideas with a holistic perspective?

2

Engage in Focused Thinking

"He did each thing as if he did nothing else."
—Spoken of Novelist Charles Dickens

Philosopher Bertrand Russell once asserted, "To be able to concentrate for a considerable time is essential to difficult achievement." Sociologist Robert Lynd observed that "knowledge is power only if a man knows what facts are not to bother about." Focused thinking removes distractions and mental clutter so that you can concentrate on an issue and think with clarity. Focused thinking can do several things for you:

1. Focused Thinking Harnesses Energy Toward a Desired Goal

Focus can bring energy and power to almost anything, whether physical or mental. If you're learning how to pitch a baseball and you want to develop a good curveball, then focused thinking while practicing will improve your technique. If you need to refine the manufacturing process of your product, focused thinking will help you develop the best method. If you want to solve a difficult mathematics problem, focused thinking helps you break through to the solution. The greater the difficulty of a problem or issue, the more focused thinking time is necessary to solve it.

2. Focused Thinking Gives Ideas Time to Develop

I love to discover and develop ideas. I often bring my creative team together for brainstorming and creative thinking. When we first get together, we try to be exhaustive in our thinking in order to generate as many ideas as possible. The birthing of a potential breakthrough often results from sharing many good ideas.

But to take ideas to the next level, you must shift from being expansive in your thinking to being selective. I have discovered that a good idea can become a great idea when it is given focus time. It's true that focusing on a single idea for a long time can be very frustrating. I've often spent days focusing on a thought and trying to develop it, only to find that I could not improve the idea. But sometimes my perseverance in focused thinking pays off. That brings me great joy. And when focused thinking is at its best, not only does the idea grow, but so do I!

3. Focused Thinking Brings Clarity to the Target

I consider golf one of my favorite hobbies. It's a wonderfully challenging game. I like it because the objectives are so clear. Professor William Mobley of the University of South Carolina made the following observation about golf:

> One of the most important things about golf is the presence of clear goals. You see the pins, you know the par—it's neither too easy nor unattainable, you know your average score, and there are competitive goals— competitive with par, with yourself and others. These goals give you something to shoot at. In work, as in golf, goals motivate.

One time on the golf course, I followed a golfer who neglected to put the pin back in the hole after he putted. Because I could not see my target, I couldn't focus properly. My focus quickly turned to frustration—and to poor play. To be a good golfer, a person needs to focus on a clear target. The same is true in thinking. Focus helps you to know the goal—and to achieve it.

4. Focused Thinking Will Take You to the Next Level

No one achieves greatness by becoming a generalist. You don't hone a skill by diluting your attention to its development. The only way to get to the next level is to focus. No matter whether your goal is to increase your level of play, sharpen your business plan, improve your bottom line, develop your subordinates, or solve personal problems, you need to focus. Author Harry A. Overstreet observed, "The immature mind hops from one thing to another; the mature mind seeks to follow through."

WHERE SHOULD YOU FOCUS YOUR THINKING?

Does every area of your life deserve dedicated, focused thinking time? Of course, the answer is no. Be selective, not exhaustive, in your focused thinking. For me, that means dedicating in-depth thinking time to four areas: leadership, creativity, communication, and intentional networking. Your choices will probably differ from mine. Here are a few suggestions to help you figure them out:

Identify Your Priorities

First, take into account your priorities—for yourself, your family, and your team. Author, consultant, and award-winning thinker Edward DeBono quipped, "A conclusion is the place where you get tired of thinking." Unfortunately, many people land on priorities based on where they run out of steam. You certainly don't want to do that. Nor do you want to let others set your agenda.

There are many ways to determine priorities. If you know yourself well, begin by focusing on your strengths, the things that make best use of your skills and God-given talents. You might also focus on what brings the highest return and reward. Do what you enjoy most and do best. You could use the 80/20 rule. Give 80 percent of your effort to the top 20 percent (most important) activities. Another way is to focus on exceptional opportunities that promise a huge return. It comes down to this: give your attention to the areas that bear fruit.

Discover Your Gifts

Not all people are self-aware and have a good handle on their own skills, gifts, and talents. They are a little like the comic strip character Charlie Brown. One day after striking out in a baseball game, he says, "Rats! I'll never be a big-league player. I just don't have it! All my life I've dreamed of playing in the big leagues, but I'll never make it."

To which Lucy replies, "Charlie Brown, you're thinking too far ahead. What you need to do is set more immediate goals for yourself."

For a moment, Charlie Brown sees a ray of hope. "Immediate goals?" he says.

"Yes," answers Lucy. "Start with the next inning. When you go out to pitch, see if you can walk out to the mound without falling down!"

I've met many individuals who grew up in a household full of Lucys. They received little encouragement or affirmation, and as a result seem at a loss for direction. If you have that kind of background, you need to work extra hard to figure out what your gifts are. Take a personality profile such as DISC or Myers-Briggs. Interview positive friends and family members to see where they think you shine. Spend some time reflecting on past successes. If you're going to focus your thinking in your areas of strength, you need to know what they are.

Develop Your Dream

If you want to achieve great things, you need to have a great dream. If you're not sure of your dream, use your focused thinking time to help you discover it. If your thinking has returned to a particular area time after time, you may be able to discover your dream there. Give it more focused time and see what happens. Once you find your dream, move forward without second-guessing. Take the advice of Satchel Paige: "Don't look back—something might be gaining on you."

The younger you are, the more likely you will give your attention to many things. That's good because if you're young you're still getting to know yourself, your strengths and weaknesses. If you focus your thinking on only one thing and your aspirations change, then you've wasted your best mental energy. As you get older and more experienced, the need to focus becomes more critical. The farther and higher you go, the more focused you can be—and need to be.

HOW CAN YOU STAY FOCUSED?

Once you have a handle on what you should think about, you must decide how to better focus on it. Here are five suggestions to help you with the process:

1. Remove Distractions

Removing distractions is no small matter in our current culture, but it's critical. How do you do it? First, by maintaining the discipline of practicing your priorities. Don't do easy things first or hard things first or urgent things first. Do first things first—the activities that give you the highest return. In that way, you keep the distractions to a minimum.

Second, insulate yourself from distractions. I've found that I need blocks of time to think without interruptions. I've mastered the art of making myself unavailable when necessary and going off to my "thinking place" so that I can work without interruptions. Because of my responsibilities as founder of three companies, however, I am always aware of the tension between my need to remain accessible to others as a leader and my need to withdraw from them to think. The best way to resolve the tension is to understand the value of both activities. Walking slowly through the crowd allows me to connect with people and know their needs. Withdrawing from the crowd allows me to think of ways to add value to them.

My advice to you is to place value on and give attention to both. If you naturally withdraw, then make sure to get out among people more often. If you're always on the go and rarely withdraw for thinking time, then remove yourself periodically so that you can unleash the potential of focused thinking. And wherever you are . . . be there!

2. Make Time for Focused Thinking

Once you have a place to think, you need the time to think. Because of the fast pace of our culture, people tend to multi-task. But that's not always a good idea. Switching from task to task can cost you up to 40 percent efficiency. According to researchers, "If you're trying to accomplish many things at the same time, you'll get more done by focusing on one task at a time, not by switching constantly from one task to another."[2]

Years ago I realized that my best thinking time occurs in the morning. Whenever possible, I reserve my mornings for thinking and writing. One way to gain time for focused thinking is to impose upon yourself a rule that one company implemented. Don't allow yourself to look at e-mail until after 10 A.M. Instead, focus your energies on your number one priority. Put non-productive time wasters on hold so that you can create thinking time for yourself.

3. Keep Items of Focus Before You

Ralph Waldo Emerson, the great transcendental thinker, believed, "Concentration is the secret of strength in politics, in war, in trade, in short in all management of human affairs." To help me concentrate on the things that matter, I work to keep important items before me. One way is to ask my assistant, Linda Eggers, to keep bringing it up, asking me about it, giving me additional information in reference to it.

I'll also keep a file or a page on my desk so that I see it every day as I work. That strategy has successfully helped me for thirty years to stimulate and sharpen ideas. If you've never done it, I recommend that you try it. (I'll tell you more about it in the section on reflective thinking.)

4. Set Goals

I believe goals are important. The mind will not focus until it has clear objectives. But the purpose of goals is to focus your attention and give you direction, not to identify a final destination. As you think about your goals, note that they should be

- Clear enough to be kept in focus
- Close enough to be achieved
- Helpful enough to change lives

Those guidelines will get you going. And be sure to write down your goals. If they're not written, I can almost guarantee that they're not focused enough. And if you *really* want to make sure they're focused, take the advice of David Belasco, who says, "If you can't write your idea on the back of my business card, you don't have a clear idea."

Even if you look back years from now and think your goals were too small, they will have served their purpose—if they provide you with direction.

5. Question Your Progress

Take a good look at yourself from time to time to see whether you are actually making progress. That is the most accurate measure of whether you are making the best use of focused thinking. Ask yourself, "Am I seeing a return for my investment of focused thinking time? Is what I am doing getting me closer to my goals? Am I headed in a direction that helps me to fulfill my commitments, maintain my priorities, and realize my dreams?"

WHAT ARE YOU GIVING UP TO GO UP?

No one can go to the highest level and remain a general-ist. My dad used to say, "Find the one thing you do well and don't do anything else." I've found that to do well at a few things, I have had to give up many things. As I worked on this chapter, I spent some time reflecting on the kinds of things I've given up. Here are the main ones:

I Can't Know Everyone

I love people, and I'm outgoing. Put me into a room full of people, and I feel energized. So it goes against my grain to restrict myself from spending time with lots of people. To compensate for that, I've done a couple of things. First, I've chosen a strong inner circle of people. They not only provide tremendous professional help, but they also make life's journey much more pleasant. Second, I ask certain friends to catch me up on what's happening in the lives of other friends. I usually do that when I'm traveling and can't block out the time I would need for focused thinking.

I Can't Do Everything

There are only a few exceptional opportunities in any person's lifetime. That's why I strive for excellence in a few things rather than a good performance in many. That's cost me. Because of my workload, I also have to skip doing many things that I would love to do. For example, every week I hand off projects that I think would be fun to do myself. I practice the 10-80-10 principle with the people to whom I'm delegating a task. I help with the first 10 percent by casting vision, laying down parameters, providing resources, and giving encouragement. Then once they've done the middle 80 percent, I come alongside them again and help them take whatever it is the rest of the way, if I can. I call it putting the cherry on top.

I Can't Go Everywhere

Every conference speaker and author has to travel a lot. Before I began doing much speaking, that seemed like a glamorous life. But after logging several million miles, I know what kind of a toll it can take. Ironically, I still love traveling for pleasure with my wife, Margaret. It's one of our great joys. She and I could take ten vacations a year and enjoy every one of them. Yet we can't, because so much of my time is consumed doing what I was called to do: help people to grow personally and to develop as leaders.

I Can't Be Well-Rounded

Being focused also keeps me from being well-rounded. I tell people, "Ninety-nine percent of everything in life I don't need to know about." I try to focus on the one percent that gives the highest return. And of the remaining ninety-nine, Margaret keeps me aware of whatever I need to know. It's one of the ways I keep from getting totally out of balance in my life.

Being willing to give up some of the things you love in order to focus on what has the greatest impact isn't an easy lesson to learn. But the earlier you embrace it, the sooner you can dedicate yourself to excellence in what matters most.

Thinking Question

Am I dedicated to removing distractions and mental clutter so that I can concentrate with clarity on the real issue?

3

Harness Creative Thinking

"The joy is in creating, not maintaining."
— Vince Lombardi, NFL Hall of Fame Coach

Creativity is pure gold, no matter what you do for a living. Annette Moser-Wellman, author of *The Five Faces of Genius*, asserts, *"The most valuable resource you bring to your work and to your firm is your creativity. More than what you get done, more than the role you play, more than your title, more than your 'output'—it's your ideas that matter."*[3] Despite the importance of a person's ability to think with creativity, few people seem to possess the skill in abundance.

If you're not as creative as you would like to be, you can change your way of thinking. Creative thinking isn't necessarily original thinking. In fact, I think people mythologize original thought. Most often, creative thinking is a composite of other thoughts discovered along the way. Even the great artists, whom we consider highly original, learned from their masters, modeled their work on that of others, and brought together a host of ideas and styles to create their own work. Study art, and you will see threads that run through the work of all artists and artistic movements, connecting them to other artists who went before them.

CHARACTERISTICS OF CREATIVE THINKERS

Perhaps you're not even sure what I mean when I ask whether you are a creative thinker. Consider some characteristics that creative thinkers have in common:

Creative Thinkers Value Ideas

Annette Moser-Wellman observes, "Highly creative people are dedicated to ideas. They don't rely on their talent alone; they rely on their discipline. Their imagination is like a second skin. They know how to manipulate it to its fullest."[4] Creativity is about having ideas—lots of them. You will have ideas only if you value ideas.

Creative Thinkers Explore Options

I've yet to meet a creative thinker who didn't love options. Exploring a multitude of possibilities helps to stimulate the imagination, and imagination is crucial to creativity. As Albert Einstein put it, "Imagination is more important than knowledge."

People who know me well will tell you that I place a very high value on options. Why? Because they provide the key to finding the best answer—not the only answer. Good thinkers come up with the best answers. They create back-up plans that provide them with alternatives. They enjoy freedom that others do not possess. And they will influence and lead others.

Creative Thinkers Embrace Ambiguity

Writer H. L. Mencken said, "It is the dull man who is always sure, and the sure man who is always dull." Creative people don't feel the need to stamp out uncertainty. They see all kinds of inconsistencies and gaps in life, and they often take delight in exploring those gaps—or in using their imagination to fill them in.

Creative Thinkers Celebrate the Offbeat

Creativity, by its very nature, often explores off of the beaten path and goes against the grain. Diplomat and long-time president of Yale University Kingman Brewster said, "There is a correlation between the creative and the screwball. So we must suffer the screwball gladly." To foster creativity in yourself or others, be willing to tolerate a little oddness.

Creative Thinkers Connect the Unconnected

Because creativity utilizes the ideas of others, there's great value in being able to connect one idea to another—especially to seemingly unrelated ideas. Graphic designer

Tim Hansen says, "Creativity is especially expressed in the ability to make connections, to make associations, to turn things around and express them in a new way."

Creating additional thoughts is like taking a trip in your car. You may know where you are going, but only as you move toward your destination can you see and experience things in a way not possible before you started. Creative thinking works something like this:

THINK ➜ COLLECT ➜ CREATE ➜ CORRECT ➜
CONNECT

Once you begin to think, you are free to collect. You ask yourself, *What material relates to this thought?* Once you have the material, you ask, *What ideas can make the thought better?* That can start to take an idea to the next level. After that, you can correct or refine it by asking, *What changes can make these ideas better?* Finally, you connect the ideas by positioning them in the right context to make the thought complete and powerful.

Creative Thinkers Don't Fear Failure

Creativity demands the ability to be unafraid of failure because creativity equals failure. You may be surprised to hear such a statement, but it's true. Charles Frankel asserts that "anxiety is the essential condition of intellectual and artistic creation." Creativity requires a willingness to look stupid. It means getting out on a limb—knowing that the limb often breaks! Creative people know these things and still keep searching for new ideas. They just don't let the ideas that *don't* work prevent them from coming up with more ideas that *do* work.

WHY YOU SHOULD DISCOVER THE JOY OF CREATIVE THINKING

Creativity can improve a person's quality of life. Here are five specific things creative thinking has the potential to do for you:

1. Creative Thinking Adds Value to Everything

Wouldn't you enjoy a limitless reservoir of ideas that you could draw upon at any time? That's what creative thinking gives you. For that reason, no matter what you are currently able to do, creativity can increase your capabilities.

Creativity is being able to see what everybody else has seen and think what nobody else has thought so that you can do what nobody else has done. Sometimes creative thinking lies along the lines of invention, where you break new ground. Other times it moves along the lines of innovation, which helps you to do old things in a new way. But either way, it's seeing the world through sufficiently new eyes so that new solutions appear. That always adds value.

2. Creative Thinking Compounds

Over the years, I've found that

Creative Thinking Is Hard Work
but
Creative Thinking Compounds Given Enough
Time and Focus

Perhaps more than any other kind of thinking, creative thinking builds on itself and increases the creativity of the thinker. Poet Maya Angelou observed, "You can't use up creativity. The more you use, the more you have. Sadly, too often creativity is smothered rather than nurtured. There has to be a climate in which new ways of thinking, perceiving, questioning are encouraged." If you cultivate creative thinking in an environment that nurtures creativity, there's no telling what kind of ideas you can come up with. (I'll talk more on that later.)

3. Creative Thinking Draws People to You and Your Ideas

Creativity is intelligence having fun. People admire intelligence, and they are always attracted to fun—so the combination is fantastic. If anyone could be said to have fun with his intelligence, it was Leonardo da Vinci. The diversity of his ideas and expertise staggers the mind. He was a painter, architect, sculptor, anatomist, musician, inventor, and engineer. The term *Renaissance man* was coined because of him.

Just as people were drawn to Da Vinci and his ideas

during the Renaissance, they are drawn to creative people today. If you cultivate creativity, you will become more attractive to other people, and they will be drawn to you.

4. Creative Thinking Helps You Learn More

Author and creativity expert Ernie Zelinski says, "Creativity is the joy of not knowing it all. The joy of not knowing it all refers to the realization that we seldom if ever have all the answers; we always have the ability to generate more solutions to just about any problem. Being creative is being able to see or imagine a great deal of opportunity to life's problems. Creativity is having options."[5]

It almost seems too obvious to say, but if you are always actively seeking new ideas, you will learn. Creativity is teachability. It's seeing more solutions than problems. And the greater the quantity of thoughts, the greater the chance for learning something new.

5. Creative Thinking Challenges the Status Quo

If you desire to improve your world—or even your own situation—then creativity will help you. The status quo and creativity are incompatible. Creativity and innovation always walk hand in hand.

HOW TO DISCOVER THE JOY OF CREATIVE THINKING

At this point you may be saying, "Okay, I'm convinced that creative thinking is important. But how do I find the creativity within me? How do I discover the joy of creative thought?" Here are five ways to do it:

1. Remove Creativity Killers

Economics professor and humor author Stephen Leacock said, "Personally, I would sooner have written *Alice in Wonderland* than the whole *Encyclopedia Britannica.*" He valued the warmth of creativity over cold facts. If you do too, then you need to eliminate attitudes that devalue creative thinking.

Take a look at the following phrases. They are almost guaranteed to kill creative thinking any time you hear (or think) them:

- I'm Not a Creative Person
- Follow the Rules
- Don't Ask Questions
- Don't Be Different
- Stay Within the Lines
- There Is Only One Way
- Don't Be Foolish
- Be Practical
- Be Serious
- Think of Your Image
- That's Not Logical

- It's Not Practical
- It's Never Been Done
- It Can't Be Done
- It Didn't Work for Them
- We Tried That Before
- It's Too Much Work
- We Can't Afford to Make a Mistake
- It Will Be Too Hard to Administer
- We Don't Have the Time
- We Don't Have the Money
- Yes, But . . .
- Play Is Frivolous
- Failure Is Final

If you think you have a great idea, don't let anyone talk you out of it even if it sounds foolish. Don't let yourself or anyone else subject you to creativity killers. After all, you can't do something new and exciting if you force yourself to stay in the same old rut. Don't just work harder at the same old thing. Make a change.

2. Think Creatively by Asking the Right Questions

Creativity is largely a matter of asking the right questions. Management trainer Sir Antony Jay said, "The uncreative mind can spot wrong answers, but it takes a creative mind to spot wrong questions." Wrong questions shut down the process of creative thinking. They direct thinkers down the same *old* path, or they chide them into believing that thinking isn't necessary at all. To stimulate creative thinking, ask yourself questions such as . . .

- Why must it be done *this* way?
- What is the root problem?
- What are the underlying issues?
- What does this remind me of?
- What is the opposite?
- What metaphor or symbol helps to explain it?
- Why is it important?
- What's the *hardest* or *most expensive* way to do it?
- Who has a different perspective on this?
- What happens if we *don't* do it at all?

You get the idea—and you can probably come up with better questions yourself. Physicist Tom Hirschfield observed, "If you don't ask, 'Why this?' often enough, somebody will ask, 'Why you?'" If you want to think creatively, you must ask good questions. You must challenge the process.

3. Develop a Creative Environment

Charlie Brower said, "A new idea is delicate. It can be killed by a sneer or a yawn; it can be stabbed to death by a quip and worried to death by a frown on the right man's brow." Negative environments kill thousands of great ideas every minute.

A creative environment, on the other hand, becomes like

a greenhouse where ideas get seeded, sprout up, and flourish. A creative environment:

- **Encourages Creativity:** David Hills says, "Studies of creativity suggest that the biggest single variable of whether or not employees will be creative is whether they perceive they have permission." When innovation and good thinking are openly encouraged and rewarded, then people see that they have permission to be creative.
- **Places a High Value on Trust among Team Members and Individuality:** Creativity always risks failure. That's why trust is so important to creative people. In the creative process, trust comes from people working together, from knowing that people on the team have experience launching successful, creative ideas, and from the assurance that creative ideas won't go to waste, because they will be implemented.
- **Embraces Those Who Are Creative:** Creative people celebrate the offbeat. How should creative people be treated? I take the advice of Tom Peters: "Weed out the dullards—nurture the nuts!" I do that by spending time with them, which I enjoy anyway. I especially like to pull people into brainstorming sessions. People look forward to an invitation to such meetings because the time will be filled with energy, ideas, and laughter. And the odds are high that a new project, seminar, or business strategy will result. When that happens, they also know a party's coming!

- **Focuses on Innovation, Not Just Invention:** Sam Weston, creator of the popular action figure GI Joe, said, "Truly groundbreaking ideas are rare, but you don't necessarily need one to make a career out of creativity. My definition of creativity is the logical combination of two or more existing elements that result in a new concept. The best way to make a living with your imagination is to develop innovative applications, not imagine completely new concepts." Creative people say, "Give me a good idea and I'll give you a better idea!"

- **Is Willing to Let People Go Outside the Lines:** Most people automatically stay within lines, even if those lines have been arbitrarily drawn or are terribly out of date. Remember, most limitations we face are not imposed on us by others; we place them on ourselves. Lack of creativity often falls into that category. If you want to be more creative, challenge boundaries. Inventor Charles Kettering said, "All human development, no matter what form it takes, must be outside the rules; otherwise, we would never have anything new." A creative environment takes that into account.

- **Appreciates the Power of a Dream:** A creative environment promotes the freedom of a dream. A creative environment encourages the use of a blank sheet of paper and the question, "If we could draw a picture of what we want to accomplish, what would that look like?" A creative environment allowed Martin Luther

King, Jr., to speak with passion and declare to millions, "I have a dream," not "I have a goal." Goals may give focus, but dreams give power. Dreams expand the world. That is why James Allen suggested that "dreamers are the saviors of the world."

The more creativity-friendly you can make your environment, the more potential it has to become creative.

4. Spend Time with Other Creative People

What if the place you work has an environment hostile to creativity, and you possess little ability to change it? One possibility is to change jobs. But what if you desire to keep working there despite the negative environment? Your best option is to find a way to spend time with other creative people.

Creativity is contagious. Have you ever noticed what happens during a good brainstorming session? One person throws out an idea. Another person uses it as a springboard to discover another idea. Someone else takes it in yet another, even better direction. Then somebody grabs hold of it and takes it to a whole new level. The interplay of ideas can be electric.

I have a strong group of creative individuals in my life. I make sure to spend regular time with them. When I leave them, I always feel energized, I'm full of ideas, and I see things differently. They truly are indispensable to my life.

It's a fact that you begin to think like the people you spend a lot of time with. The more time you can spend with creative people engaging in creative activities, the more creative you will become.

5. Get Out of Your Box

Actress Katharine Hepburn remarked, "If you obey all the rules . . . you will miss all the fun." While I don't think it's necessary to break all the rules (many are in place to protect us), I do think it's unwise to allow self-imposed limitations to hinder us. Creative thinkers know that they must repeatedly break out of the "box" of their own history and personal limitations in order to experience creative breakthroughs.

The most effective way to help yourself get out of the box is to expose yourself to new paradigms. One way you can do that is by traveling to new places. Explore other cultures, countries, and traditions. Find out how people very different from you live and think. Another is to read on new subjects. I'm naturally curious and love to learn, but I still have a tendency to read books only on my favorite subjects, such as leadership. I sometimes have to force myself to read books that broaden my thinking, because I know it's worth it. If you want to break out of your own box, get into somebody's else's. Read broadly.

Many people mistakenly believe that if individuals aren't born with creativity, they will never be creative. But you can see from the many strategies and examples I've given that creativity can be cultivated in the right supportive environment.

Thinking Question

Am I working to break out of my "box" of limitations so that I explore ideas and options to experience creative breakthroughs?

4

Employ Realistic Thinking

"The first responsibility of a leader is to define reality."
—MAX DEPREE, CHAIRMAN EMERITUS
OF HERMAN MILLER, INC.

As anyone knows who's been out of school for a few years, there's usually a huge gap between a college education and the reality of the working world. Honestly, early in my career, I went out of my way to avoid too much realistic thinking because I thought it would interfere with my creative thinking. But as I've grown, I've come to realize that realistic thinking adds to my life.

REALITY CHECK

Reality is the difference between what we wish for and what is. It took some time for me to evolve into a realistic thinker. The process went in phases. First, I did not engage in realistic thinking at all. After a while, I realized that it was necessary, so I began to engage in it occasionally. (But I didn't like it because I thought it was too negative. And any time I could delegate it, I did.) Eventually, I found that I *had* to engage in realistic thinking if I was going to solve problems and learn from my mistakes. And in time, I became willing to think realistically *before* I got in trouble and make it a continual part of my life. Today, I encourage my key leaders to think realistically. We make realistic thinking the foundation of our business because we derive certainty and security from it.

WHY YOU SHOULD RECOGNIZE THE IMPORTANCE OF REALISTIC THINKING

If you're a naturally optimistic person, as I am, you may not possess great desire to become a more realistic thinker. But cultivating the ability to be realistic in your thinking will not undermine your faith in people, nor will it lessen your ability to see and seize opportunities. Instead, it will add value to you in other ways:

1. Realistic Thinking Minimizes Downside Risk

Actions always have consequences; realistic thinking helps you to determine what those consequences could be. And that's crucial, because only by recognizing and considering consequences can you plan for them. If you plan for the worst-case scenario, you can minimize the downside risk.

2. Realistic Thinking Gives You a Target and Game Plan

I've known businesspeople who were not realistic thinkers. Here's the good news: they were very positive and had a high degree of hope for their business. Here's the bad news: hope is not a strategy.

Realistic thinking leads to excellence in leadership and management because it requires people to face reality. They begin to define their target and develop a game plan to hit it. When people engage in realistic thinking, they also begin to simplify practices and procedures, which results in better efficiency.

Truthfully, in business only a few decisions are important. Realistic thinkers understand the difference between the important decisions and those that are merely necessary in the normal course of business. The decisions that matter relate directly to your purpose. James Allen was right when he wrote, "Until thought is linked with purpose there is no intelligent accomplishment."[6]

3. Realistic Thinking Is a Catalyst for Change

People who rely on hope for their success rarely make change a high priority. If you have only hope, you imply that achievement and success are out of your hands. It's a matter of luck or chance. Why bother changing?

Realistic thinking can dispel that kind of wrong attitude. There's nothing like staring reality in the face to make a person recognize the need for change. Change alone doesn't bring growth but you cannot have growth without change.

4. Realistic Thinking Provides Security

Any time you have thought through the worst that can happen and you have developed contingency plans to meet it, you become more confident and secure. It's reassuring to know that you are unlikely to be surprised. Disappointment is the difference between expectations and reality. Realistic thinking minimizes the difference between the two.

5. Realistic Thinking Gives You Credibility

Realistic thinking helps people to buy in to the leader and his or her vision. Leaders continually surprised by the unexpected soon lose credibility with their followers. On the other hand, leaders who think realistically and plan accordingly position their organizations to win. That gives their people confidence in them.

The best leaders ask realistic questions *before* casting vision. They ask themselves things like . . .

- Is it possible?
- Does this dream include everyone or just a few?
- Have I identified and articulated the areas that will make this dream difficult to achieve?

6. Realistic Thinking Provides a Foundation to Build On

Thomas Edison observed, "The value of a good idea is in using it." The bottom line on realistic thinking is that it helps you to make an idea usable by taking away the "wish" factor. Most ideas and efforts don't accomplish

their intended results because they rely too much on what
we wish rather than what is.

You can't build a house in midair; it needs a solid foundation. Ideas and plans are the same. They need something
concrete on which to build. Realistic thinking provides that
solid foundation.

7. Realistic Thinking Is a Friend to Those in Trouble

If creativity is what you would do if you were unafraid of
the possibility of failure, then reality is dealing with failure
if it does happen. Realistic thinking gives you something
concrete to fall back on during times of trouble, which can
be very reassuring. Certainty in the midst of uncertainty
brings stability.

8. Realistic Thinking Brings the Dream to Fruition

British novelist John Galsworthy wrote, "Idealism increases in direct proportion to one's distance from the
problem." If you don't get close enough to a problem, you
can't tackle it. If you don't take a realistic look at your
dream—and what it will take to accomplish it—you will
never achieve it. Realistic thinking helps to pave the way
for bringing any dream to fruition.

HOW TO RECOGNIZE THE IMPORTANCE OF
REALISTIC THINKING

Because I'm naturally optimistic rather than realistic,
I've had to take concrete steps to improve my thinking in

this area. Here are five things I do to improve my realistic thinking:

1. Develop an Appreciation for Truth

I could not develop as a realistic thinker until I gained an appreciation for realistic thinking. And that means learning to look at and enjoy truth. President Harry S. Truman said, "I never give 'em hell. I just tell the truth and they think it is hell." That's the way many people react to truth. People tend to exaggerate their success and minimize their failures or deficiencies. They live according to Ruckert's Law, believing there is nothing so small that it can't be blown out of proportion.

Unfortunately, many people today could be described by a quote from Winston Churchill: "Men occasionally stumble over the truth, but most pick themselves up and hurry off as if nothing has happened." More recently, television journalist Ted Koppel observed, "Our society finds truth too strong a medicine to digest undiluted. In its purest form, truth is not a polite tap on the shoulder. It is a howling reproach." In other words, the truth will set you free—but first it will make you angry! If you want to become a realistic thinker, however, you need to get comfortable dealing with the truth and face up to it.

2. Do Your Homework

The process of realistic thinking begins with doing your homework. You must first get the facts. Former governor, congressman, and ambassador Chester Bowles said,

"When you approach a problem, strip yourself of preconceived opinions and prejudice, assemble and learn the facts of the situation, make the decision which seems to you to be the most honest, and then stick to it." It doesn't matter how sound your thinking is if it's based on faulty data or assumptions. You can't think well in the absence of facts (or in the presence of poor information).

You can also find out what others have done in similar circumstances. Remember, your thinking doesn't necessarily have to be original; it just has to be solid. Why not learn all that you can from good thinkers who have faced similar situations in the past? Some of my best thinking has been done by others!

3. Think Through the Pros and Cons

There's nothing like taking the time to really examine the pros and cons of an issue to give you a strong dose of reality. It rarely comes down to simply choosing the course of action with the greatest number of pros, because all pros and cons do not carry equal weight. But that's not the value of the exercise, anyway. Rather, it helps you to dig into the facts, examine an issue from many angles, and really count the cost of a possible course of action.

4. Picture the Worst-Case Scenario

The essence of realistic thinking is discovering, picturing, and examining the worst-case scenario. Ask yourself questions such as:

- What if sales fall short of projections?
- What if revenue hits rock bottom? (Not an optimist's rock bottom, but real rock bottom!)
- What if we don't win the account?
- What if the client doesn't pay us?
- What if we have to do the job short-handed?
- What if our best player gets sick?
- What if all the colleges reject my application?
- What if the market goes belly up?
- What if the volunteers quit?
- What if nobody shows up?

You get the idea. The point is that you need to think about worst-case possibilities whether you are running a business, leading a department, pastoring a church, coaching a team, or planning your personal finances. Your goal isn't to be negative or to expect the worst, just to be ready for it in case it happens. That way, you give yourself the best chance for a positive result—no matter what.

If you picture the worst case and examine it honestly, then you really have experienced a reality check. You're ready for anything. As you do that, take the advice of Charles Hole, who advised, "Deliberate with caution, but act with decision; and yield with graciousness or oppose with firmness."

5. Align Your Thinking with Your Resources

One of the keys to maximizing realistic thinking is aligning your resources with your objectives. Looking at pros and cons and examining worst-case scenarios will make you aware of any gaps between what you desire and what really is. Once you know what those gaps are, you can use your resources to fill them. After all, that's what resources are for.

SUPER BOWL, SUPER DOME, SUPER SECURITY

Our country received lessons in realistic thinking following the tragedy of September 11, 2001. The destruction of the World Trade Center buildings in New York City far surpassed any worst-case scenarios that anyone might have envisioned. In the wake of that event, we now find that we don't have the luxury of avoiding or neglecting realistic thinking.

I was reminded of that on Sunday, February 3, 2002, when I attended the Super Bowl in New Orleans, Louisiana. I had been to the big game twice before, to root for the home team—first San Diego and later Atlanta—and had seen both teams lose! But I had never been to a game like this. The occasion had been designated a National Security Special Event. That meant that the U.S. Secret Service would be overseeing it; military personnel would work with local law enforcement; and security would be of the highest caliber. The Secret Service brought in several hundred agents and secured the area. In preparation for the game, access to the Super Dome was highly restricted, with intensified screening. Officials blocked off roads, closed the nearby interstate, and designated the area a no-fly zone.

We arrived early at the dome—officials suggested fans arrive up to five hours ahead of game time—and we immediately saw evidence of the precautionary measures. Eight-foot fences surrounded the whole area, and concrete barriers prevented unauthorized vehicles from getting close to the building. We could see sharpshooters positioned at various locations, including on the roof of some adjacent buildings. When we reached a gate, police officers and security personnel patted us down and examined everyone's belongings. After that they directed us to go through metal detectors. Only then did they allow us into the stadium.

"That's all well and good," you may be saying, "but what would have happened had there been a terrorist attack?" The Secret Service had that covered too, because they had prepared for the worst-case scenario. Evacuation plans had been put into place, and personnel at the Super Dome had been drilled to make sure everyone knew what to do in case of an emergency.

New Orleans mayor Marc Morial said the day before the Super Bowl, "We want to send a message to all visitors that New Orleans is going to be the safest place in America."[7] We got the message. We didn't feel the least bit worried. That's what happens when leaders recognize the importance of realistic thinking.

Thinking Question

Am I building a solid mental foundation on facts so that I can think with certainty?

5

Utilize Strategic Thinking

"Most people spend more time planning their summer vacation than planning their lives."

—Source Unknown

When you hear the words "strategic thinking," what comes to mind? Do visions of business plans dance in your head? Do you conjure up marketing plans, the kind that can turn a company around? Perhaps you contemplate global politics. Or you recall some of history's greatest military campaigns: Hannibal crossing the Alps to surprise the Roman army, Charlemagne's conquest of Western Europe, or the Allies' D-Day invasion of Normandy. Perhaps, but strategy doesn't have to be restricted to military action—or even to business. Strategic thinking can make a positive impact on any area of life.

PLAN YOUR LIFE, LIVE YOUR PLAN

I've observed that most people try to plan their lives one day at a time. They wake up, make up their to-do list, and dive into action (although some people aren't even *that* strategic).

Fewer individuals plan their lives one week at a time. They review their calendar for the week, check their appointments, review their goals, and then get to work. They generally outachieve most of their daily-planning colleagues. I try to take planning one step further.

At the beginning of every month, I spend half a day working on my calendar for the next forty days. Forty days works for me rather than just thirty. That way, I get a jump on the next month and don't get surprised. I begin by reviewing my travel schedule and planning activities with my family. Then I review what projects, lessons, and other objectives I want to accomplish during those five to six weeks. Then I start blocking out days and times for thinking, writing, working, meeting with people, etc. I set times to do fun things, such as seeing a show, watching a ball game, or playing golf. I also set aside small blocks of time to compensate for the unexpected. By the time I'm done, I can tell you nearly everything I'll be doing, almost hour by hour, during the coming weeks. This strategy is one of the reasons I have been able to accomplish much.

WHY YOU SHOULD RELEASE THE POWER OF STRATEGIC THINKING

Strategic thinking helps me to plan, to become more efficient, to maximize my strengths, and to find the most direct path toward achieving any objective. The benefits of strategic thinking are numerous. Here are a few of the reasons you should adopt it as one of your thinking tools:

1. Strategic Thinking Simplifies the Difficult

Strategic thinking is really nothing more than planning on steroids. Spanish novelist Miguel de Cervantes said, "The man who is prepared has his battle half fought." Strategic thinking takes complex issues and long-term objectives, which can be very difficult to address, and breaks them down into manageable sizes. Anything becomes simpler when it has a plan!

Strategic thinking can also help you simplify the management of everyday life. I do that by using systems, which are nothing more than good strategies repeated. I am well known among pastors and other speakers for my filing system. Writing a lesson or speech can be difficult. But because I use my system to file quotes, stories, and articles, when I need something to flesh out or illustrate a point, I simply go to one of my 1,200 files and find a good piece of material that works. Just about any difficult task can be made simpler with strategic thinking.

2. Strategic Thinking Prompts You to Ask the Right Questions

Do you want to break down complex or difficult issues? Then ask questions. Strategic thinking forces you through this process. Take a look at the following questions developed by my friend Bobb Biehl, the author of *Masterplanning*.[8]

- **Direction:** What should we do next? Why?
- **Organization:** Who is responsible for what? Who is responsible for whom? Do we have the right people in the right places?
- **Cash:** What is our projected income, expense, net? Can we afford it? How can we afford it?
- **Tracking:** Are we on target?
- **Overall Evaluation:** Are we achieving the quality we expect and demand of ourselves?
- **Refinement:** How can we be more effective and more efficient (move toward the ideal)?

These may not be the only questions you need to ask to begin formulating a strategic plan, but they are certainly a good start.

3. Strategic Thinking Prompts Customization

General George S. Patton observed, "Successful generals make plans to fit circumstances, but do not try to create circumstances to fit plans."

All good strategic thinkers are precise in their thinking. They try to match the strategy to the problem, because strategy isn't a one-size-fits-all proposition. Sloppy or generalized thinking is an enemy of achievement. The intention to customize in strategic thinking forces a person to go beyond vague ideas and engage in specific ways to go after a task or problem. It sharpens the mind.

4. Strategic Thinking Prepares You Today for an Uncertain Tomorrow

Strategic thinking is the bridge that links where you are to where you want to be. It gives direction and credibility today and increases your potential for success tomorrow. It is, as Mary Webb suggests, like saddling your dreams before you ride them.

5. Strategic Thinking Reduces the Margin of Error

Any time you shoot from the hip or go into a totally reactive mode, you increase your margin for error. It's like a golfer stepping up to a golf ball and hitting it before lining up the shot. Misaligning a shot by just a few degrees can send the ball a hundred yards off target. Strategic thinking, however, greatly reduces that margin for error. It lines up your actions with your objectives, just as lining up a shot in golf helps you to put the ball closer to the pin. The better aligned you are with your target, the better the odds that you will be going in the right direction.

6. Strategic Thinking Gives You Influence with Others

One executive confided in another: "Our company has a short range plan and a long range plan. Our short range plan is to stay afloat long enough to make it to our long range plan." That's hardly a strategy, yet that's the position where some business leaders put themselves. There's more than one problem with neglecting strategic thinking in that way. Not only does it fail to build the business, but it also loses the respect of everyone involved with the business.

The one with the plan is the one with the power. It doesn't matter in what kind of activity you're involved. Employees want to follow the business leader with a good business plan. Volunteers want to join the pastor with a good ministry plan. Children want to be with the adult who has the well-thought-out vacation plan. If you practice strategic thinking, others will listen to you and they will want to follow you. If you possess a position of leadership in an organization, strategic thinking is essential.

HOW TO RELEASE THE POWER OF STRATEGIC THINKING

To become a better strategic thinker able to formulate and implement plans that will achieve the desired objective, take the following guidelines to heart:

1. Break Down the Issue

The first step in strategic thinking is to break down an issue into smaller, more manageable parts so that you can focus on them more effectively. How you do it is not as important as just doing it. You might break an issue down by function. That's what automotive innovator Henry Ford did when he created the assembly line, and that's why he said, "Nothing is particularly hard if you divide it into small jobs."

How you break down an issue is up to you, whether it's

by function, timetable, responsibility, purpose, or some other method. The point is that you need to break it down. Only one person in a million can juggle the whole thing in his head and think strategically to create solid, viable plans.

2. Ask Why Before How

When most people begin using strategic thinking to solve a problem or plan a way to meet an objective, they often make the mistake of jumping the gun and trying immediately to figure out *how* to accomplish it. Instead of asking *how*, they should first ask *why*. If you jump right into problem solving mode, how are you going to know all the issues?

Eugene G. Grace says, "Thousands of engineers can design bridges, calculate strains and stresses, and draw up specifications for machines, but the great engineer is the man who can tell whether the bridge or the machine should be built at all, where it should be built, and when." Asking why helps you to think about all the reasons for decisions. It helps you to open your mind to possibilities and opportunities. The size of an opportunity often determines the level of resources and effort that you must invest. Big opportunities allow for big decisions. If you jump to *how* too quickly, you might miss that.

3. Identify the Real Issues and Objectives

William Feather, author of *The Business of Life*, said, "Before it can be solved, a problem must be clearly defined." Too many people rush to solutions, and as a result they end up solving the wrong problem. To avoid that, ask probing questions to expose the real issues. Challenge all of your assumptions. Collect information even after you think you've identified the issue. (You may still have to act with incomplete data, but you don't want to jump to a conclusion before you gather enough information to begin identifying the real issue.) Begin by asking, *What else could be the real issue?* You should also remove any personal agenda. More than almost anything else, that can cloud your judgment. Discovering your real situation and objectives is a major part of the battle. Once the real issues are identified, the solutions are often simple.

4. Review Your Resources

I already mentioned how important it is to be aware of your resources, but it bears repeating. A strategy that doesn't take into account resources is doomed to failure. Take an inventory. How much time do you have? How much money? What kinds of materials, supplies, or inventory do you have? What are your other assets? What liabilities or obligations will come into play? Which people on the team can make an impact? You know your own organization and profession. Figure out what resources you have at your disposal.

5. Develop Your Plan

How you approach the planning process depends greatly on your profession and the size of the challenge that you're planning to tackle, so it's difficult to recommend many specifics. However, no matter how you go about planning, take this advice: start with the obvious. When you tackle an issue or plan that way, it brings unity and consensus to the team, because everyone sees those things. Obvious elements build mental momentum and initiate creativity and intensity. The best way to create a road to the complex is to build on the fundamentals.

6. Put the Right People in the Right Place

It's critical that you include your team as part of your strategic thinking. Before you can implement your plan, you must make sure that you have the right people in place. Even the best strategic thinking won't help if you don't take into account the people part of the equation. Look at what happens if you miscalculate:

Wrong Person: Problems instead of Potential
Wrong Place: Frustration instead of Fulfillment
Wrong Plan: Grief instead of Growth

Everything comes together, however, when you put together all three elements: the right person, the right place, and the right plan.

7. Keep Repeating the Process

My friend Olan Hendrix remarked, "Strategic thinking is like showering, you have to keep doing it." If you expect to solve any major problem once, you're in for disappointment. Little things can be won easily through systems and personal discipline. But major issues need major strategic thinking time. What Thane Yost said is really true: "The will to win is worthless if you do not have the will to prepare." If you want to be an effective strategic thinker, then you need to become a continuous strategic thinker.

As I was working on this chapter, I came across an article in my local paper on the celebration of the Jewish Passover and how millions of American Jews read the order of service for their Seder, or Passover meal, from a small booklet produced by Maxwell House Coffee. For more than seventy years, the coffee company has produced the booklet, called a Haggada, and during those years it has distributed more than 40 million copies of it.

"I remember using them all my life," said Regina Witt, who is in her fifties. So does her mother, who is almost ninety. "It's our tradition. I think it would be very strange not to use them."[9]

So how did Maxwell House come to supply the booklets? It was the result of strategic thinking. Eighty years ago, marketing man Joseph Jacobs advised that the company could sell coffee during Passover if the product were certified Kosher by a rabbi. (Since 1923, Maxwell House coffee has been certified Kosher for Passover.) And then Jacobs suggested that if they gave away the Haggada booklets, they could increase sales.[10] They've been creating the booklets—and selling coffee during Passover—ever since. That's what can happen when you unleash the power of strategic thinking.

Thinking Question

Am I implementing strategic plans that give me direction for today and increase my potential for tomorrow?

6

Explore Possibility Thinking

"Nothing is so embarrassing as watching someone do something that you said could not be done."

—SAM EWING

People who embrace possibility thinking are capable of accomplishing tasks that seem impossible because they believe in solutions. Here are several reasons why you should become a possibility thinker:

1. Possibility Thinking Increases Your Possibilities

When you believe you can do something difficult—and you succeed—many doors open for you. When George Lucas succeeded in making *Star Wars*, despite those who said the special effects he wanted hadn't ever been done and couldn't be done, many other possibilities opened up to him. Industrial Light and Magic (ILM), the company he created to produce those "impossible" special effects, became a source of revenue to help underwrite his other projects. He was able to produce merchandising tie-ins to his movies, thus bringing in another revenue stream to fund his movie making. But his confidence in doing the difficult has also made a huge impact on other movie makers and a whole new generation of movie goers. Popular culture writer Chris Salewicz asserts, "At first directly through his own work and then via the unparalleled influence of ILM, George Lucas has dictated for two decades the essential broad notion of what is cinema."[11] If you open yourself up to possibility thinking, you open yourself up to many other possibilities.

2. Possibility Thinking Draws Opportunities and People to You

The case of George Lucas helps you to see how being a possibility thinker can create new opportunities and attract people. People who think big attract big people to them. If you want to achieve big things, you need to become a possibility thinker.

3. Possibility Thinking Increases Others' Possibilities

Big thinkers who make things happen also create possibilities for others. That happens, in part, because it's contagious. You can't help but become more confident and think bigger when you're around possibility thinkers.

4. Possibility Thinking Allows You to Dream Big Dreams

No matter what your profession, possibility thinking can help you to broaden your horizons and dream bigger dreams. Professor David J. Schwartz believes, "Big thinkers are specialists in creating positive forward-looking, optimistic pictures in their own minds and in the minds of others." If you embrace possibility thinking, your dreams will go from molehill to mountain size, and because you believe in possibilities, you put yourself in position to achieve them.

5. Possibility Thinking Makes It Possible to Rise Above Average

During the 1970s, when oil prices went through the roof, automobile makers were ordered to make their cars more fuel efficient. One manufacturer asked a group of senior engineers to drastically reduce the weight of cars they were designing. They worked on the problem and searched for solutions, but they finally concluded that making lighter cars couldn't be done, would be too expensive, and would present too many safety concerns. They couldn't get out of the rut of their average thinking.

What was the auto maker's solution? They gave the problem to a group of less-experienced engineers. The new group found ways to reduce the weight of the company's automobiles by hundreds of pounds. Because they thought that solving the problem was possible, it was. Every time you remove the label of impossible from a task, you raise your potential from average to off the charts.

6. Possibility Thinking Gives You Energy

A direct correlation exists between possibility thinking and the level of a person's energy. Who gets energized by

the prospect of losing? If you know something can't succeed, how much time and energy are you willing to give it?
Nobody goes looking for a lost cause. You invest yourself
in what you believe can succeed. When you embrace possibility thinking, you believe in what you're doing, and that
gives you energy.

7. Possibility Thinking Keeps You from Giving Up

Above all, possibility thinkers believe they can succeed.
Denis Waitley, author of *The Psychology of Winning*, says,
"The winners in life think constantly in terms of 'I can, I
will and I am.' Losers, on the other hand, concentrate their
waking thoughts on what they should have done, or what
they don't do." If you believe you can't do something, then
it doesn't matter how hard you try, because you've already
lost. If you believe you can do something, you have already
won much of the battle.

One of the people who showed himself to be a great
possibility thinker in 2001 was New York mayor Rudy
Giuliani. In the hours following the World Trade Center
tragedy, Giuliani not only led the city through the chaos
of the disaster, but he instilled confidence in everyone he
touched. Afterward, he gave some insight and perspective
on his experience:

I was so proud of the people I saw on the street. No
chaos, but they were frightened and confused, and it
seemed to me that they needed to hear from my heart
where I thought we were going. I was trying to think,

Where can I go for some comparison to this, some lessons about how to handle it? So I started thinking about Churchill, started thinking that we're going to have to rebuild the spirit of the city, and what better example than Churchill and the people of London during the Blitz in 1940, who had to keep up their spirit during this sustained bombing? It was a comforting thought.[12]

Sixteen hours after the planes struck the buildings in New York City, when Giuliani finally returned at 2:30 A.M. to his apartment for a rest, instead of sleeping, he read the World War II chapters of *Churchill: A Biography* by Roy Jenkins. He learned how Winston Churchill helped his people to see the possibilities and kept his people going. Inspired, Giuliani did the same for his own people six decades later.

HOW TO FEEL THE ENERGY OF POSSIBILITY THINKING

If you are a naturally positive person who already embraces possibility thinking, then you're already tracking with me. However, some people, rather than being optimistic, are naturally negative or cynical. They believe that possibility thinkers are naïve or foolish. If your thinking runs toward pessimism, let me ask you a question: how many highly successful people do you know who are continually negative? How many impossibility thinkers are you acquainted with who achieve big things? None!

People with an it-can't-be-done mindset have two choices. They can expect the worst and continually experience it; or they can change their thinking. That's what George Lucas did. Believe it or not, even though he is a possibility thinker, he is not a naturally positive person. He says, "I'm very cynical, and as a result, I think the defense I have against it is to be optimistic."[13] In other words, he chooses to think positively. He sums it up this way: "As corny as it sounds, the power of positive thinking goes a long way. So determination and positive thinking combined with talent combined with knowing your craft . . . that may sound like a naïve point of view, but at the same time it's worked for me and it's worked for all my friends—so I have come to believe it."[14]

If you want possibility thinking to work for you, then begin by following these suggestions:

1. Stop Focusing on the Impossibilities

The first step in becoming a possibility thinker is to stop yourself from searching for and dwelling on what's wrong with any given situation. Sports psychologist Bob Rotella recounts, "I tell people: If you don't want to get into positive thinking, that's OK. Just eliminate all the negative thoughts from your mind, and whatever's left will be fine."

If possibility thinking is new to you, you're going to have to give yourself a lot of coaching to eliminate some of the negative self-talk you may hear in your head. When you automatically start listing all the things that can go wrong or all the reasons something can't be done, stop yourself and say, "Don't go there." Then ask, "What's right about this?" That will help to get you started. And if negativity is a really big problem for you and pessimistic things come out of your mouth before you've even thought them through, you may need to enlist the aid of a friend or family member to alert you every time you utter negative ideas.

2. Stay Away from the "Experts"

So-called experts do more to shoot down people's dreams than just about anybody else.

Possibility thinkers are very reluctant to dismiss anything as impossible. Rocket pioneer Wernher von Braun said, "I have learned to use the word impossible with the greatest of caution." And Napoleon Bonaparte declared, "The word impossible is not in my dictionary." If you feel you must take the advice of an expert, however, then heed the words of John Andrew Holmes, who asserted, "Never tell a young person that something cannot be done. God may have been waiting centuries for somebody ignorant enough of the impossible to do that thing." If you want to achieve something, give yourself permission to believe it is possible—no matter what experts might say.

3. Look for Possibilities in Every Situation

Becoming a possibility thinker is more than just refusing to let yourself be negative. It's something more. It's looking for positive possibilities despite the circumstances. I recently heard Don Soderquist, former president of Wal-Mart, tell a wonderful story that illustrates how a person can find positive possibilities in any situation. Soderquist had gone with Sam Walton to Huntsville, Alabama, to open several new stores. While there, Walton suggested they visit the competition. Here's what Soderquist said happened:[15]

We went into one [store], and I have to tell you that it was the worst store I've ever seen in my life. It was terrible. There were no customers. There was no help on the floor. The aisles were cluttered with merchandise, empty shelves, dirty, it was absolutely terrible. He [Walton] walked one way and I'd walk the other way and we'd kind of meet out on the sidewalk. He said, "What'd you think, Don?"

I said, "Sam, that is the absolutely worst store I've ever seen in my life. I mean, did you see the aisles?"

He said, "Don, did you see the pantyhose rack?"

I said, "No, I didn't, Sam. I must have gone on a different aisle than you. I didn't see that."

He said, "That was the best pantyhose rack I've ever seen, Don." And he said, "I pulled the fixture out and on the back was the name of the manufacturer. When we get back, I want you to call that manufacturer and have him come in and visit with our fixture people. I want to put that rack in our stores. It's absolutely the best I've ever seen." And he said next, "Did you see the ethnic cosmetics?"

I said, "Sam, that must have been right next to the pantyhose rack, because I absolutely missed that."

He said, "Don, do you realize that in our stores we

have four feet of ethnic cosmetics. These people had 12 feet of it. We are absolutely missing the boat. I wrote down the distributor of some of those products. When we get back, I want you to get a hold of our cosmetic buyer and get these people in. We absolutely need to expand our ethnic cosmetics."

Now, Sam Walton didn't hit me on the head and say, "Don, now what lesson did you learn from this?" He had already hit me on the head by looking for the good, looking how to improve, striving for excellence. It's so easy to go and look at what other people do badly. But one of the leadership characteristics of vision that he showed me, and I'll never forget it, is look for the good in what other people are doing and apply it.

It doesn't take a genius IQ or twenty years of experience to find the possibility in every situation. All it takes is the right attitude, and anybody can cultivate that.

4. Dream One Size Bigger

One of the best ways to cultivate a possibility mind-set is to prompt yourself to dream one size bigger than you normally do. Let's face it: most people dream too small. They don't think big enough. Henry Curtis advises, "Make your plans as fantastic as you like, because twenty-five years from now, they will seem mediocre. Make your plans ten times as great as you first planned, and twenty-five years from now you will wonder why you did not make them fifty times as great."

If you push yourself to dream more expansively, to imagine your organization one size bigger, to make your goals at least a step beyond what makes you comfortable, you will be forced to grow. And it will set you up to believe in greater possibilities.

5. Question the Status Quo

Most people want their lives to keep improving, yet they value peace and stability at the same time. People often forget that you can't improve and still stay the same. Growth means change. Change requires challenging the status quo. If you want greater possibilities, you can't settle for what you have now. When you become a possibility thinker, you will face many people who will want you to give up your dreams and embrace the status quo. Achievers refuse to accept the status quo.

As you begin to explore greater possibilities for yourself, your organization, or your family—and others challenge you for it—take comfort in knowing that *right now* as you read this, other possibility thinkers across the country and around the world are thinking about curing cancer, developing new energy sources, feeding hungry people, and improving quality of life. They are challenging the status quo against the odds—and you should, too.

6. Find Inspiration from Great Achievers

You can learn a lot about possibility thinking by studying great achievers. I mentioned George Lucas in this chapter. Perhaps he doesn't appeal to you, or you don't like the movie industry. (Personally, I'm not a big science fiction fan, but I admire Lucas as a thinker, creative visionary, and business-person.) Find some achievers you admire and study them. Look for people with the attitude of Robert F. Kennedy, who popularized George Bernard Shaw's stirring statement: "Some men see things as they are and say, 'Why?' I dream of things that never were and say, 'Why not?'"

I know possibility thinking isn't in style with many people. So call it what you like: the will to succeed, belief in yourself, confidence in your ability, faith. It's really true: people who believe they can't, don't. But if you believe you can, you can! That's the power of possibility thinking.

Thinking Question

Am I unleashing the enthusiasm of possibility thinking to find solutions for even seemingly impossible situations?

7

Learn from Reflective Thinking

*"To doubt everything or to believe everything are two
equally convenient solutions; both dispense with the ne-
cessity of reflection."*

—JULES HENRI POINCARÉ

The pace of our society does not encourage reflective
thinking. Most people would rather act than think. Now,
don't get me wrong. I'm a person of action. I have very high
energy and I like to see things accomplished. But I'm also a
reflective thinker. Reflective thinking is like the Crock-Pot
of the mind. It encourages your thoughts to simmer until
they're done. As I go through this process, my goal is to
reflect so that I might learn from my successes and mistakes, discover what I should try to repeat, and determine
what I should change. It is always a valuable exercise. By
mentally visiting past situations, you can think with greater
understanding.

1. Reflective Thinking Gives You True Perspective

When our children were young and still lived at home, we used to take them on wonderful vacations every year. When we got home, they always knew that I was going to ask them two questions: "What did you like best?" and "What did you learn?" It didn't matter whether we went to Walt Disney World or Washington, D.C.

I always asked those questions. Why? Because I wanted them to reflect on their experiences. Children don't naturally grasp the value (or cost) of an experience unless prompted. They take things for granted. I wanted my children to appreciate our trips and to learn from them. When you reflect, you are able to put an experience into perspective. You are able to evaluate its timing. And you are able to gain a new appreciation for things that before went unnoticed. Most people are able to recognize the sacrifices of their parents or other people only when they become parents themselves. That's the kind of perspective that comes with reflection.

2. Reflective Thinking Gives Emotional Integrity to Your Thought Life

Few people have good perspective in the heat of an emotional moment. Most individuals who enjoy the thrill of an experience try to go back and recapture it without first trying to evaluate it. (It's one of the reasons our culture produces so many thrill seekers.) Likewise, those who survive a traumatic experience usually avoid similar situations at all costs, which sometimes ties them into emotional knots.

Reflective thinking enables you to distance yourself

from the intense emotions of particularly good or bad experiences and see them with fresh eyes. You can see the thrills of the past in the light of emotional maturity and examine tragedies in the light of truth and logic. That process can help a person to stop carrying around a bunch of negative emotional baggage.

President George Washington observed, "We ought not to look back unless it is to derive useful lessons from past errors, and for the purpose of profiting by dearly bought experience." Any feeling that can stand up to the light of truth and can be sustained over time has emotional integrity and is therefore worthy of your mind and heart.

3. Reflective Thinking Increases Your Confidence in Decision-making

Have you ever made a snap judgment and later wondered if you did the right thing? Everybody has. Reflective thinking can help to diffuse that doubt. It also gives you confidence for the next decision. Once you've reflected on an issue, you don't have to repeat every step of the thinking process when you're faced with it again. You've got mental road markers from having been there before. That compresses and speeds up thinking time—and it gives you confidence. And over time, it can also strengthen your intuition.

4. Reflective Thinking Clarifies the Big Picture

When you engage in reflective thinking, you can put ideas and experiences into a more accurate context. Reflective thinking encourages us to go back and spend time pondering what we have done and what we have seen. If a person who loses his job reflects on what happened, he may see a pattern of events that led to his dismissal. He will better understand what happened, why it happened, and what things were his responsibility. If he also looks at the incidents that occurred afterward, he may realize that in the larger scheme of things, he's better off in his new position because it better fits his skills and desires. Without reflection, it can be very difficult to see that big picture.

5. Reflective Thinking Takes a Good Experience and Makes It a Valuable Experience

When you were just starting out in your career, did it seem that few people were willing to give someone without experience an opportunity? At the same time, could you see people who had been on their jobs twenty years who yet did their work poorly? If so, that probably frustrated you. Playwright William Shakespeare wrote, "Experience is a jewel, and it had need be so, for it is often purchased at an infinite rate." Yet, experience alone does not add value to a life. It's not necessarily experience that is valuable; it's the insight people gain because of their experience. Reflective thinking turns experience into insight.

Mark Twain said, "We should be careful to get out of an experience all the wisdom that is in it—not like the cat that sits down on a hot stove lid. She will never sit down on a hot stove lid again—and that is well; but also she will never sit down on a cold one anymore."[16] An experience becomes valuable when it informs or equips us to meet new experiences. Reflective thinking helps to do that.

HOW TO EMBRACE THE LESSONS
OF REFLECTIVE THINKING

If you are like most people in our culture today, you probably do very little reflective thinking. If that's the case, it may be holding you back more than you think. Take to heart the following suggestions to increase your ability to think reflectively:

1. Set Aside Time for Reflection

Greek philosopher Socrates observed, "The unexamined life is not worth living." For most people, however, reflection and self-examination doesn't come naturally. It can be a fairly uncomfortable activity for a variety of reasons: they have a hard time staying focused; they find the process dull; or they don't like spending a lot of time thinking about emotionally difficult issues. But if you don't carve out the time for it, you are unlikely to do any reflective thinking.

2. Remove Yourself from Distractions

As much as any other kind of thinking, reflection requires solitude. Distraction and reflection simply don't mix. It's not the kind of thing you can do well near a television, in a cubicle, while the phone is ringing, or with children in the same room.

One of the reasons I've been able to accomplish much and keep growing personally is that I've not only set aside time to reflect, but I've separated myself from distractions for short blocks of time: thirty minutes in the spa; an hour outside on a rock in my backyard; or a few hours in a comfortable chair in my office. The place doesn't matter—as long as you remove yourself from distractions and interruptions.

3. Regularly Review Your Calendar or Journal

Most people use their calendar as a planning tool, which it is. But few people use it as a reflective thinking tool. What could be better, however, for helping you to review where you have been and what you have done—except maybe a journal? I'm not a journaler in the regular sense; I don't use writing to figure out what I'm thinking and feeling. Instead, I figure out what I'm thinking and feeling, and then I write down significant thoughts and action points. (I file the thoughts so that I can quickly put my hands on them again. I immediately execute the action points or delegate them to someone else.)

Calendars and journals remind you of how you've spent your time, show you whether your activities match your priorities, and help you see whether you are making progress. They also offer you an opportunity to recall activities that you might not have had the time to reflect on previously. Some of the most valuable thoughts you've ever had may have been lost because you didn't give yourself the reflection time you needed.

4. Ask the Right Questions

The value you receive from reflecting will depend on the kinds of questions you ask yourself. The better the questions, the more gold you will mine from your thinking.

When I reflect, I think in terms of my values, relationships, and experiences. Here are some sample questions:

- **Personal Growth:** What have I learned today that will help me grow? How can I apply it to my life? When should I apply it?
- **Adding Value:** To whom did I add value today? How do I know I added value to that person? Can I follow up and compound the positive benefit he or she received?
- **Leadership:** Did I lead by example today? Did I lift my people and organization to a higher level? What did I do and how did I do it?
- **Personal Faith:** Did I represent God well today? Did I practice the Golden Rule? Have I "walked the second mile" with someone?
- **Marriage and Family:** Did I communicate love to my family today? How did I show that love? Did they feel it? Did they return it?
- **Inner Circle:** Have I spent enough time with my key players? What can I do to help them be more successful? In what areas can I mentor them?
- **Discoveries:** What did I encounter today to which I need to give more thinking time? Are there lessons to be learned? Are there things to be done?

How you organize your reflection time is up to you. You may want to adapt my pattern to your own values. Or you can try a system that my friend Dick Biggs uses. He creates three columns on a sheet of paper:

Year   Turning Point   Impact

This system is good for reflecting on the bigger picture. Dick used it to see patterns in his life, such as when he moved to Atlanta and was encouraged by a new teacher to write. You could just as easily write "Event," "Significance," and "Action Point" on a page to help you benefit from reflective thinking. The main thing is to create questions that work for you, and write down any significant thoughts that come to you during the reflection time.

5. Cement Your Learning Through Action

Writing down the good thoughts that come out of your reflective thinking has value, but nothing helps you to grow like putting your thoughts into action. To do that, you must be intentional. When you read a good book, for example, there are always good thoughts, quotes, or lessons that you can take away from it and use yourself. I always mark the takeaways in a book and then reread them when I'm done with the book. When I listen to a message, I record the takeaways so that I can file them for future use. When I go to a seminar, I take good notes, and I use a system of symbols to cue me to do certain things:

- An arrow like this ➡ means to look at this material again.

- An asterisk like this * next to a marked section means to file it according to the subject noted.
- A bracket like this [means that I want to use what's marked in a lecture or book.
- An arrow like this ⬆ means this idea will take off if I work at it.

When most people go to a conference or seminar, they enjoy the experience, listen to the speakers, and sometimes even take notes. But nothing happens after they go home. They like many of the concepts they hear, but when they close their notebooks, they don't think about them again. When that happens, they receive little more than a temporary surge of motivation. When you go to a conference, revisit what you heard, reflect on it, and then put it into action; it can change your life.

Ultimately, reflective thinking has three main values: it gives me perspective within context; it allows me to continually connect with my journey; and it provides counsel and direction concerning my future. It is an invaluable tool to my personal growth. Few things in life can help me learn and improve the way reflective thinking can.

Thinking Question

Am I regularly revisiting the past to gain a true perspective and think with understanding?

8

Question Popular Thinking

"I'm not an answering machine, I'm a questioning machine. If we have all the answers, how come we're in such a mess?"

—Douglas Cardinal

Economist John Maynard Keynes, whose ideas profoundly influenced economic theory and practices in the twentieth century, asserted, "The difficulty lies not so much in developing new ideas as in escaping from the old ones." Going against popular thinking can be difficult, whether you're a businessperson bucking company tradition, a pastor introducing new types of music to his church, a new mother rejecting old wives' tales handed down from her parents, or a teenager ignoring currently popular styles.

Many of the ideas in this book go against popular thinking. If you value popularity over good thinking, then you will severely limit your potential to learn the types of thinking encouraged by this book.

Popular thinking is . . .
- Too Average to Understand the Value of Good Thinking,
- Too Inflexible to Realize the Impact of Changed Thinking,
- Too Lazy to Master the Process of Intentional Thinking,
- Too Small to See the Wisdom of Big-picture Thinking,
- Too Satisfied to Unleash the Potential of Focused Thinking,
- Too Traditional to Discover the Joy of Creative Thinking,
- Too Naïve to Recognize the Importance of Realistic Thinking,
- Too Undisciplined to Release the Power of Strategic Thinking,
- Too Limiting to Feel the Energy of Possibility Thinking,
- Too Trendy to Embrace the Lessons of Reflective Thinking,
- Too Shallow to Question the Acceptance of Popular Thinking,
- Too Proud to Encourage the Participation of Shared Thinking,

- Too Self-absorbed to Experience the Satisfaction of Unselfish Thinking, and
- Too Uncommitted to Enjoy the Return of Bottom-Line Thinking.

If you want to become a good thinker, then start preparing yourself for the possibility of becoming unpopular.

WHY YOU SHOULD QUESTION THE ACCEPTANCE OF POPULAR THINKING

I've given you some broad reasons for questioning the acceptance of popular thinking. Now allow me to be more specific:

1. Popular Thinking Sometimes Means Not Thinking

My friend Kevin Myers sums up the idea of popular thinking by saying, "The problem with popular thinking is that it doesn't require you to think at all." Good thinking is hard work. If it were easy, everybody would be a good thinker. Unfortunately, many people try to live life the easy way. They don't want to do the hard work of thinking or pay the price of success. It's easier to do what other people do and hope that *they* thought it out.

Look at the stock market recommendations of some experts. By the time they publish their picks, most are following a trend, not creating one or even riding its crest. The people who are going to make money on the stocks they recommend have already done so by the time the general public hears about it. When people blindly follow a trend, they're not doing their own thinking.

2. Popular Thinking Offers False Hope

Benno Muller-Hill, a professor in the University of Cologne genetics department, tells how one morning in high school he stood last in a line of forty students in the schoolyard. His physics teacher had set up a telescope so that his students could view a planet and its moons. The first student stepped up to the telescope. He looked through it, but when the teacher asked if he could see anything, the boy said no; his nearsightedness hampered his view. The teacher showed him how to adjust the focus, and the boy finally said he could see the planet and moons. One by one, the students stepped up to the telescope and saw what they were supposed to see. Finally, the second to last student looked into the telescope and announced that he could not see anything.

"You idiot," shouted the teacher, "you have to adjust the lenses."

The student tried, but he finally said, "I still can't see anything. It is all black."

The teacher, disgusted, looked through the telescope himself, and then looked up with a strange expression. The lens cap still covered the telescope. None of the students had been able to see anything![17]

Many people look for safety and security in popular thinking. They figure that if a lot of people are doing something, then it must be right. It must be a good idea.

If most people accept it, then it probably represents fairness, equality, compassion, and sensitivity, right? Not necessarily. Popular thinking said the earth was the center of the universe, yet Copernicus studied the stars and planets and proved mathematically that the earth and the other planets in our solar system revolved around the sun. Popular thinking said surgery didn't require clean instruments, yet Joseph Lister studied the high death rates in hospitals and introduced antiseptic practices that immediately saved lives. Popular thinking said that women shouldn't have the right to vote, yet people like Emmeline Pankhurst and Susan B. Anthony fought for and won that right. Popular thinking put the Nazis into power in Germany, yet Hitler's regime murdered millions and nearly destroyed Europe. We must always remember there is a huge difference between acceptance and intelligence. People may say that there's safety in numbers, but that's not always true.

Sometimes it's painfully obvious that popular thinking isn't good and right. Other times it's less evident. For example, consider the staggering number of people in the United States who have run up large amounts of debt on their credit cards. Anyone who is financially astute will tell you that's a bad idea. Yet millions follow right along with the popular thinking of buy now, pay later. And so they pay, and pay, and pay. Many promises of popular thinking ring hollow. Don't let them fool you.

3. Popular Thinking Is Slow to Embrace Change

Popular thinking loves the status quo. It puts its confidence in the idea of the moment, and holds on to it with all its might. As a result, it resists change and dampens innovation. Donald M. Nelson, former president of the Society of Independent Motion Picture Producers, criticized popular thinking when he asserted, "We must discard the idea that past routine, past ways of doing things, are probably the best ways. On the contrary, we must assume that there is probably a better way to do almost everything. We must stop assuming that a thing which has never been done before probably cannot be done at all."

4. Popular Thinking Brings Only Average Results

The bottom line? Popular thinking brings mediocre results. Here is popular thinking in a nutshell:

Popular = Normal = Average

It's the least of the best and the best of the least. We limit our success when we adopt popular thinking. It represents putting in the least energy to just get by. You must reject common thinking if you want to accomplish uncommon results.

HOW TO QUESTION THE ACCEPTANCE OF POPULAR THINKING

Popular thinking has often proved to be wrong and limiting. Questioning it isn't necessarily hard, once you cultivate the habit of doing so. The difficulty is in getting started. Begin by doing the following things:

1. Think Before You Follow

Many individuals follow others almost automatically. Sometimes they do so because they desire to take the path of least resistance. Other times they fear rejection. Or they believe there's wisdom in doing what everyone else does. But if you want to succeed, you need to think about what's best, not what's popular.

Challenging popular thinking requires a willingness to be unpopular and go outside of the norm. Following the tragedy of September 11, 2001, for example, few people willingly chose to travel by plane. But that was the best time to travel: crowds were down, security was up, and airlines were cutting prices. About a month after the tragedy, my wife, Margaret, and I heard that Broadway shows had lots of seats and many New York hotel rooms remained empty. Popular thinking said, stay away from New York. We used that as an opportunity. We got cheap plane tickets to the city, booked a room in a great hotel for about half price, and got tickets to the most sought-after show: *The Producers*. As we took our seats in the theater, we sat next to a woman beside herself with excitement.

"I can't believe I'm finally here," she said to us. "I've waited so long. This is the best show on Broadway—and the hardest to get tickets to." Then she turned to look me in the eye and said, "I've had my tickets for a year and a half, waiting to see this show. How long ago did you get yours?"

"You won't like my answer," I replied.

"Oh, come on," she said. "How long?"

"I got mine five days ago," I answered. She looked at us in horror. By the way, she was right. It's one of the best shows we've seen in a while. And we got to see it only because we were willing to go against popular thinking when everyone else was staying at home.

As you begin to think against the grain of popular thinking, remind yourself that

- Unpopular thinking, even when resulting in success, is largely underrated, unrecognized, and misunderstood.
- Unpopular thinking contains the seeds of vision and opportunity.
- Unpopular thinking is required for all progress.

The next time you feel ready to conform to popular thinking on an issue, stop and think. You may not want to create change for its own sake, but you certainly don't want to blindly follow just because you haven't thought about what's best.

2. Appreciate Thinking Different from Your Own

One of the ways to embrace innovation and change is to learn to appreciate how others think. To do that, you must continually expose yourself to people different from yourself. My brother, Larry Maxwell—a good businessman and an innovative thinker—continually challenges popular thinking by thinking differently. He says:

> Most of our people in sales and middle management come from businesses with products and services different from ours. That constantly exposes us to new ways of thinking. We also discourage our people from active participation in formal business and trade associations and fraternities because their thinking is quite common. They don't need to spend lots of time thinking the way everyone else in the industry does.

As you strive to challenge popular thinking, spend time with people with different backgrounds, education levels, professional experiences, personal interests, etc. You will think like the people with whom you spend the most time. If you spend time with people who think out of the box, you're more likely to challenge popular thinking and break new ground.

3. Continually Question Your Own Thinking

Let's face it, any time we find a way of thinking that works, one of our greatest temptations is to go back to it repeatedly, even if it no longer works well. The greatest enemy to tomorrow's success is sometimes today's success. My friend Andy Stanley recently taught a leadership lesson at INJOY's Catalyst Conference called "Challenging the Process." He described how progress must be preceded by change, and he pointed out many of the dynamics involved in questioning popular thinking. In an organization, he said, we should remember that every tradition was originally a good idea—and perhaps even revolutionary. But every tradition may not be a good idea for the future.

In your organization, if you were involved in putting into place what currently exists, then it's likely that you will resist change—even change for the better. That's why it's important to challenge your own thinking. If you're too attached to your own thinking and how everything is done now, then nothing will change for the better.

4. Try New Things in New Ways

When was the last time you did something for the first time? Do you avoid taking risks or trying new things? One of the best ways to get out of the rut of your own thinking is to innovate. You can do that in little, everyday ways: drive to work a different way from normal. Order an unfamiliar dish at your favorite restaurant. Ask a different colleague to help you with a familiar project. Take yourself off of autopilot.

Unpopular thinking asks questions and seeks options. In 1997, my three companies moved to Atlanta, Georgia. It's a great city, but traffic at peak times can get crazy. Immediately after moving here, I began looking for and testing alternative routes to desired destinations so that I would not be caught in traffic. From my house to the airport, for example, I have discovered and used nine routes within eight miles and twelve minutes from one another. Often I am amazed to see people sitting on the freeway when they could be moving forward on an alternative route. What is the problem? Too many people have not tried new things in new ways. It is true: most people are more satisfied with old problems than committed to finding new solutions.

How you go about doing new things in new ways is not as important as making sure you do it. (Besides, if you try to do new things in the same way that everyone else does, are you really going against popular thinking?) Get out there and do something different today.

5. Get Used to Being Uncomfortable

When it comes right down to it, popular thinking is comfortable. It's like an old recliner adjusted to all the owner's idiosyncrasies. The problem with most old recliners is that no one has *looked* at them lately. If so, they'd agree that it's time to get a new one! If you want to reject popular thinking in order to embrace achievement, you'll have to get used to being uncomfortable.

If you embrace unpopular thinking and make decisions based upon what works best and what is right rather than what is commonly accepted, know this: in your early years you won't be as wrong as people think you are. In your later years, you won't be as right as people think you are. And all through the years, you will be better than you thought you could be.

Thinking Question

Am I consciously rejecting the limitations of common thinking in order to accomplish uncommon results?

9

Benefit from Shared Thinking

"None of us is as smart as all of us."

—KEN BLANCHARD

Good thinkers, especially those who are also good leaders, understand the power of shared thinking. They know that when they value the thoughts and ideas of others, they receive the compounding results of shared thinking and accomplish more than they ever could on their own.

Those who participate in shared thinking understand the following:

1. Shared Thinking Is Faster than Solo Thinking

We live in a truly fast-paced world. To function at its current rate of speed, we can't go it alone. I think the generation of young men and women just entering the workforce sense that very strongly. Perhaps that is why they value community so highly and are more likely to work for a company they like than one that pays them well. Working with others is like giving yourself a shortcut.

If you want to learn a new skill quickly, how do you do it? Do you go off by yourself and figure it out, or do you get someone to show you how? You can always learn more quickly from someone with experience—whether you're trying to learn how to use a new software package, develop your golf swing, or cook a new dish.

2. Shared Thinking Is More Innovative than Solo Thinking

We tend to think of great thinkers and innovators as soloists, but the truth is that the greatest innovative thinking doesn't occur in a vacuum. Innovation results from collaboration. Albert Einstein once remarked, "Many times a day I realize how much my own outer and inner life is built upon the labors of my fellow men, both living and dead, and how earnestly I must exert myself in order to give in return as much as I have received."

Shared thinking leads to greater innovation, whether you look at the work of researchers Marie and Pierre Curie, surrealists Luis Brunel and Salvador Dali, or songwriters John Lennon and Paul McCartney. If you combine your thoughts with the thoughts of others, you will come up with thoughts you've never had!

3. Shared Thinking Brings More Maturity than Solo Thinking

As much as we would like to think that we know it all, each of us is probably painfully aware of our blind spots and areas of inexperience. When I first started out as a pastor, I had dreams and energy, but little experience. To try to overcome that, I attempted to get several high-profile pastors of growing churches to share their thinking with me. In the early 1970s, I wrote letters to the ten most successful pastors in the country, offering them what was a huge amount of money to me at the time ($100) to meet me for an hour, so that I could ask them questions. When one said yes, I'd visit him. I didn't talk much, except to ask a few questions. I wasn't there to impress anyone or satisfy my ego. I was there to learn. I listened to everything he said, took careful notes, and absorbed everything I could. Those experiences changed my life.

You've had experiences I haven't, and I've had experiences you haven't. Put us together and we bring a broader range of personal history—and therefore maturity—to the table. If you don't have the experience you need, hook up with someone who does.

4. Shared Thinking Is Stronger than Solo Thinking

Philosopher-poet Johann Wolfgang von Goethe said, "To accept good advice is but to increase one's own ability." Two heads are better than one—when they are thinking in the same direction. It's like harnessing two horses to pull a wagon. They are stronger pulling together than either is individually. But did you know that when they pull together, they can move more weight than the sum of what they can move individually? A synergy comes from working together. That same kind of energy comes into play when people think together.

5. Shared Thinking Returns Greater Value than Solo Thinking

Because shared thinking is stronger than solo thinking, it's obvious that it yields a higher return. That happens because of the compounding action of shared thinking. But it also offers other benefits. The personal return you receive from shared thinking and experiences can be great. Clarence Francis sums up the benefits in the following observation: "I sincerely believe that the word relationships is the key to the prospect of a decent world. It seems abundantly clear that every problem you will have—in your family, in your work, in our nation, or in this world—is essentially a matter of relationships, of interdependence."

6. Shared Thinking Is the Only Way to Have Great Thinking

I believe that every great idea begins with three or four good ideas. And most good ideas come from shared thinking. Playwright Ben Jonson said, "He that is taught only by himself has a fool for a master."

When I was in school, teachers put the emphasis on being right and on doing better than the other students, rarely on working together to come up with good answers. Yet all the answers improve when they make the best use of everyone's thinking. If we each have one thought, and together we have two thoughts, then we always have the potential for a great thought.

HOW TO ENCOURAGE THE PARTICIPATION OF SHARED THINKING

Some people naturally participate in shared thinking. Any time they see a problem, they think, *Who do I know who can help with this?* Leaders tend to be that way. So do extroverts. However, you don't have to be either of those to benefit from shared thinking. Use the following steps to help you improve your ability to harness shared thinking:

1. Value the Ideas of Others

First, believe that the ideas of other people have value. If you don't, your hands will be tied. How do you know if you truly want input from others? Ask yourself these questions:

- **Am I emotionally secure?** People who lack confidence and worry about their status, position, or power tend to reject the ideas of others, protect their turf, and keep people at bay. It takes a secure person to consider others' ideas. Years ago, an emotionally insecure person took a key position on my board of directors. After a couple of meetings, it became obvious to the other board members that this individual would not positively contribute to the organization. I asked a seasoned leader on the board, "Why does this person always do and say things that hinder our progress?" I'll never forget his reply: "Hurting people hurt people."

- **Do I place value on people?** You won't value the ideas of a person if you don't value and respect the person himself or herself. Have you ever considered your conduct around people you value, versus those you don't? Look at the differences:

If I Value People	If I Don't Value People
I want to spend time with them	I don't want to be around them
I listen to them	I neglect to listen
I want to help them	I don't offer them help
I am influenced by them	I ignore them
I respect them	I am indifferent

- **Do I value the interactive process?** A wonderful synergy often occurs as the result of shared thinking. It can take you places you've never been. Publisher Malcolm Forbes asserted, "Listening to advice often accomplishes far more than heeding it." I must say, I didn't always value shared thinking. For many years, I tended to withdraw when I wanted to develop ideas. Only reluctantly did I work on ideas with others. When a colleague challenged me on this, I started to analyze my hesitancy. I realized that it went back to my college experience. Some days in the classroom I could tell that a teacher was unprepared to lecture and instead spent the class time asking us to give our uninformed opinions on a subject. Most of the time, the opinions seemed no better than mine. I had come to class so that the professor could teach me. I realized that the process of sharing ideas wasn't the problem; it was *who* was doing the talking. Shared thinking is only as good as the people doing the sharing. Since learning that lesson, I have embraced the interactive process, and now I believe it is one of my strengths. Still, I always think about whom I bring around the table for a shared thinking session. (I'll tell you my guidelines for whom I invite later in this chapter.)

You must open yourself up to the *idea* of sharing ideas before you will engage in the *process* of shared thinking.

2. Move from Competition to Cooperation

Jeffrey J. Fox, author of *How to Become CEO*, says, "Always be on the lookout for ideas. Be completely indiscriminate as to the source. Get ideas from customers, children, competitors, other industries, or cab drivers. It doesn't matter who thought of an idea."[18]

A person who values cooperation desires to complete the ideas of others, not compete with them. If someone asks you to share ideas, focus on helping the team, not getting ahead personally. And if you are the one who brings people together to share their thoughts, praise the idea more than the source of the idea. If the best idea always wins (rather than the person who offered it), then all will share their thoughts with greater enthusiasm.

3. Have an Agenda When You Meet

I enjoy spending time with certain people, whether we discuss ideas or not: my wife, Margaret; my children; my grandchildren; my parents. Though we often do discuss ideas, it doesn't bother me if we don't; we are family. When I spend time with nearly anyone else in my life, however, I have an agenda. I know what I want to accomplish.

The more I respect the wisdom of the person, the more I listen. For example, when I meet with someone I'm mentoring, I let the person ask the questions, but I expect to do most of the talking. When I meet with someone who mentors me, I mostly keep my mouth shut. In other relationships, the give and take is more even. But no matter with whom I meet, I have a reason for getting together and I have an expectation for what I'll give to it and get from it. That's true whether it's for business or pleasure.

4. Get the Right People Around the Table

To get anything of value out of shared thinking, you need to have people around who bring something to the table. As you prepare to ask people to participate in shared thinking, use the following criteria for the selection process. Choose . . .

- People whose greatest desire is the success of the ideas.
- People who can add value to another's thoughts.
- People who can emotionally handle quick changes in the conversation.

- People who appreciate the strengths of others in areas where they are weak.
- People who understand their place of value at the table.
- People who place what is best for the team before themselves.
- People who can bring out the best thinking in the people around them.
- People who possess maturity, experience, and success in the issue under discussion.
- People who will take ownership and responsibility for decisions.
- People who will leave the table with a "we" attitude, not a "me" attitude.

Too often we choose our brainstorming partners based on feelings of friendship or circumstances or convenience. But that doesn't help us to discover and create the ideas of the highest order. Who we invite to the table makes all the difference.

5. Compensate Good Thinkers and Collaborators Well

Successful organizations practice shared thinking. If you lead an organization, department, or team, then you can't afford to be without people who are good at shared thinking. As you recruit and hire, look for good thinkers who value others, have experience with the collaborative process, and are emotionally secure. Then pay them well and challenge them to use their thinking skills and share their ideas often. Nothing adds value like a lot of good thinkers putting their minds together.

No matter what you're trying to accomplish, you can do it better with shared thinking. That is why I spend much of my life teaching leadership. Good leadership helps to put together the right people at the right time for the right purpose so that everybody wins. All it takes is the right people and a willingness to participate in shared thinking.

Thinking Question

Am I consistently including the heads of others to think "over my head" and achieve compounding results?

10

Practice Unselfish Thinking

"We cannot hold a torch to light another's path without brightening our own."

—Ben Sweetland

So far in this book, we've discussed many kinds of thinking that can help you to achieve more. Each of them has the potential to make you more successful. Now I want to acquaint you with a kind of thinking with the potential to change your life in another way. It might even redefine how you view success.

Unselfish thinking can often deliver a return greater than any other kind of thinking. Take a look at some of its benefits:

1. Unselfish Thinking Brings Personal Fulfillment

Few things in life bring greater personal rewards than helping others. Charles H. Burr believed, "Getters generally don't get happiness; givers get it." Helping people brings great satisfaction. When you spend your day unselfishly serving others, at night you can lay down your head with no regrets and sleep soundly. In *Bringing Out the Best in People*, Alan Loy McGinnis remarked, "There is no more noble occupation in the world than to assist another human being—to help someone succeed."

Even if you have spent much of your life pursuing selfish gain, it's never too late to have a change of heart. Even the most miserable person, like Charles Dickens's Scrooge, can turn his life around and make a difference for others. That's what Alfred Nobel did. When he saw his own obituary in the newspaper (his brother had died and the editor had written about the wrong Nobel, saying that the explosives his company produced had killed many people), Nobel vowed to promote peace and acknowledge contributions to humanity. That is how the Nobel Prizes came into being.

2. Unselfish Thinking Adds Value to Others

In 1904, Bessie Anderson Stanley wrote the following definition of success in *Brown Book* magazine:

He has achieved success who has lived well, laughed often and loved much; who has enjoyed the trust of pure women, the respect of intelligent men and the love of little children, who has filled his niche and accomplished his task; who has left the world better than he found it, whether by an improved poppy, a perfect poem, or a rescued soul; who has never lacked appreciation of earth's beauty or failed to express it, who has always looked for the best in others and given them the best he had, whose life was an inspiration, whose memory a benediction.

When you get outside of yourself and make a contribution to others, you really begin to live.

3. Unselfish Thinking Encourages Other Virtues

When you see a four-year-old, you expect to observe selfishness. But when you see it in a forty-year-old, it's not very attractive, is it?

Of all the qualities a person can pursue, unselfish thinking seems to make the biggest difference toward cultivating other virtues. I think that's because the ability to give unselfishly is so difficult. It goes against the grain of human nature. But if you can learn to think unselfishly and become a giver, then it becomes easier to develop many other virtues: gratitude, love, respect, patience, discipline, etc.

4. Unselfish Thinking Increases Quality of Life

The spirit of generosity created by unselfish thinking gives people an appreciation for life and an understanding of its higher values. Seeing those in need and giving to meet that need puts a lot of things into perspective. It increases the quality of life of the giver and the receiver. That's why I believe that

There is no life as empty as the self-centered life.
There is no life as centered as the self-empty life.

If you want to improve your world, then focus your attention on helping others.

5. Unselfish Thinking Makes You Part of Something Greater than Yourself

Merck and Company, the global pharmaceutical corporation, has always seen itself as doing more than just producing products and making a profit. It desires to serve humanity. In the mid-1980s, the company developed a drug to cure river blindness, a disease that infects and causes blindness in millions of people, particularly in developing countries. While it was a good product, potential customers couldn't afford to buy it. So what did Merck do? It developed the drug anyway, and in 1987 announced that it would give the medicine free to anyone who needed it. As of 1998, the company had given more than 250 million tablets away.[19]

George W. Merck says, "We try never to forget that medicine is for the people. It is not for the profits. The profits follow, and if we have remembered that, they have never failed to appear." The lesson to be learned? Simple. Instead of trying to be great, be part of something greater than yourself.

6. Unselfish Thinking Creates a Legacy

Jack Balousek, president and chief operating officer of True North Communications, says, "Learn, earn, return— these are the three phases of life. The first third should be devoted to education, the second third to building a career and making a living, and the last third to giving back to others—returning something in gratitude. Each state seems to be a preparation for the next one."

If you are successful, it becomes possible for you to leave an inheritance *for* others. But if you desire to do more, to create a legacy, then you need to leave that *in* others. When you think unselfishly and invest in others, you gain the opportunity to create a legacy that will outlive you.

HOW TO EXPERIENCE THE SATISFACTION OF UNSELFISH THINKING

I think most people recognize the value of unselfish thinking, and most would even agree that it's an ability they would like to develop. Many people, however, are at a loss concerning how to change their thinking. To begin cultivating the ability to think unselfishly, I recommend that you do the following:

1. Put Others First

The process begins with realizing that everything is not about you! That requires humility and a shift in focus. In *The Power of Ethical Management*, Ken Blanchard and Norman Vincent Peale wrote, "People with humility don't think less of themselves; they just think of themselves less." If you want to become less selfish in your thinking, then you need to stop thinking about your wants and begin focusing on others' needs. Paul the Apostle exhorted, "Do nothing out of selfish ambition or vain conceit, but in humility consider others better than yourselves. Each of you should look not only to your own interests, but also to the interests of others."[20] Make a mental and emotional commitment to look out for the interests of others.

2. Expose Yourself to Situations Where People Have Needs

It's one thing to believe you are willing to give unselfishly. It's another to actually do it. To make the transition, you need to put yourself in a position where you can see people's needs and do something about it.

The kind of giving you do isn't important at first. You can serve at your church, make donations to a food bank, volunteer professional services, or give to a charitable organization. The point is to learn how to give and to cultivate the habit of thinking like a giver.

3. Give Quietly or Anonymously

Once you have learned to give of yourself, then the next step is to learn to give when you cannot receive anything in return. It's almost always easier to give when you receive recognition for it than it is when no one is likely to know about it. The people who give in order to receive a lot of fanfare, however, have already received any reward they will get. There are spiritual, mental, and emotional benefits that come only to those who give anonymously. If you've never done it before, try it.

4. Invest in People Intentionally

The highest level of unselfish thinking comes when you

give of yourself to another person for that person's personal development or well-being. If you're married or a parent, you know this from personal experience. What does your spouse value most highly: money in the bank or your time freely given? What would small children really rather have from you: a toy or your undivided attention? The people who love you would rather have you than what you can give them.

If you want to become the kind of person who invests in people, then consider others and their journey so that you can collaborate with them. Each relationship is like a partnership created for mutual benefit. As you go into any relationship, think about how you can invest in the other person so that it becomes a win-win situation. Here is how relationships most often play out:

I win, you lose—I win only once.

You win, I lose—You win only once.

We both win—We win many times.

We both lose—Good-bye, partnership!

The best relationships are win-win. Why don't more people go into relationships with that attitude? I'll tell you why: most people want to make sure that they win first. Unselfish thinkers, on the other hand, go into a relationship and make sure that the other person wins first. And that makes all the difference.

5. Continually Check Your Motives

François de la Rochefoucauld said, "What seems to be

generosity is often no more than disguised ambition, which overlooks a small interest in order to secure a great one." The hardest thing for most people is fighting their natural tendency to put themselves first. That's why it's important to continually examine your motives to make sure you're not sliding backward into selfishness.

Do you want to check your motives? Then follow the modeling of Benjamin Franklin. Every day, he asked himself two questions. When he got up in the morning, he would ask, "What good am I going to do today?" And before he went to bed, he would ask, "What good have I done today?" If you can answer those questions with selflessness and integrity, you can keep yourself on track.

GIVE WHILE YOU LIVE

In the fall of 2001, we all witnessed a demonstration of unselfish thinking unlike anything we had seen in the United States for many years. Who can forget the events of September 11, 2001? I had just finished teaching a leadership lesson when my assistant, Linda Eggers, came into the studio to announce the tragic news. Like most Americans, I remained riveted to the television all day and heard the reports of the firefighters and police officers who raced into the World Trade Center towers to help others, never worrying about their own safety.

In the days following the tragedy, millions of Americans expressed a great desire to do something that would help the situation. I had the same desire. My company was scheduled to do a training via simulcast on September 15, the Saturday following the tragedy. Our leadership team decided to add a one-and-a-half-hour program titled "America Prays" to the end of the simulcast. In it, my friend Max Lucado wrote and read a prayer, expressing the heart's cry of millions. Franklin Graham prayed for our national leaders. Jim and Shirley Dobson gave advice to parents on how to help their children deal with the event. And Bruce Wilkinson and I asked the simulcast viewers to give financially to the people injured on September 11. Amazingly, they gave $5.9 million, which World Vision graciously agreed to distribute to those in need. Unselfish thinking and giving turned a very dark hour into one of light and hope.

Less than two weeks after the tragedy, I was able to travel to Ground Zero in New York City. I went to view the site of the destruction, to thank the men and women clearing away the wreckage, and to pray for them. I can't really do justice to what I saw. I've traveled to New York dozens of times. It's one of my favorite places in the world. My wife and I had been up in the towers with our children many times before and have wonderful memories of that area. To look at the place where the buildings had once stood and to see nothing but rubble, dust, and twisted metal—it's simply indescribable.

What many Americans didn't realize is that for many months people worked diligently to clean up the site. Many were New York City firefighters and other city workers. Others were volunteers. They worked around the clock, seven days a week. And when they came across the remains of someone in the rubble, they called for silence and reverently carried them out.

Since I am a clergyman, I was asked to wear a clerical collar upon entering the area. As I walked around, many workers saw the collar and asked me to pray for them. It was a humbling privilege.

American educator Horace Mann said, "Be ashamed to die until you have won some victory for humanity." According to this standard, New York City's firefighters are certainly prepared for death. The service they perform is often truly heroic. You and I may never be required to lay down our lives for others, as they did. But we can give to others in different ways. We can be unselfish thinkers who put others first and add value to their lives. We can work with them so that they go farther than they thought possible.

Thinking Question

Am I continually considering others and their journey in order to think with maximum collaboration?

11

Rely on Bottom-Line Thinking

"There ain't no rules around here. We're trying to accomplish something."

— THOMAS EDISON, INVENTOR

How do you figure out the bottom line for your organization, business, department, team, or group? In many businesses, the bottom line is literally the bottom line. Profit determines whether you are succeeding. But dollars should not always be the primary measure of success. Would you measure the ultimate success of your family by how much money you had at the end of the month or year? And if you run a non-profit or volunteer organization, how would you know whether you were performing at your highest potential? How do you think bottom line in that situation?

A NONPROFIT'S BOTTOM LINE

Frances Hesselbein had to ask herself exactly that question in 1976, when she became the national executive director of the Girl Scouts of America. When she first got involved with the Girl Scouts, running the organization was the last thing she expected. She and her husband, John, were partners in Hesselbein Studios, a small family business that filmed television commercials and promotional films. She wrote the scripts and he made the films. In the early 1950s, she was recruited as a volunteer troop leader at the Second Presbyterian Church in Johnstown, Pennsylvania. Even that was unusual, since she had a son and no daughters. But she agreed to do it on a temporary basis. She must have loved it, because she led the troop for nine years!

In time, she became council president and a member of the national board. Then she served as executive director of the Talus Rock Girl Scout Council, a full-time paid position. By the time she took the job as CEO of the national organization, the Girl Scouts was in trouble. The organization lacked direction, teenage girls were losing interest in scouting, and it was becoming increasingly difficult to recruit adult volunteers, especially with greater numbers of women entering the workforce. Meanwhile, the Boy Scouts was considering opening itself to girls. Hesselbein desperately needed to bring the organization back to the bottom line.

"We kept asking ourselves very simple questions," she says. "What is our business? Who is our customer? And what does the customer consider value? If you're the Girl Scouts, IBM, or AT&T, you have to manage for a mission."[21] Hesselbein's focus on mission enabled her to identify the Girl Scouts' bottom line. "We really are here for one reason: to help a girl reach her highest potential. More than any one thing, that made the difference. Because when you are clear about your mission, corporate goals and operating objectives flow from it."[22]

Once she figured out her bottom line, she was able to create a strategy to try to achieve it. She started by reorganizing the national staff. Then she created a planning system to be used by each of the 350 regional councils. And she introduced management training to the organization. Hesselbein didn't restrict herself to changes in leadership and organization. In the 1960s and '70s, the country had changed and so had its girls—but the Girl Scouts hadn't. Hesselbein tackled that issue, too. The organization made its activities more relevant to the current culture, giving greater opportunities for use of computers, for example, rather than hosting a party. She also sought out minority participation, created bilingual materials, and reached out to low-income households. If helping girls reach their highest potential was the group's bottom line, then why not be more aggressive helping girls who traditionally have fewer opportunities? The strategy worked beautifully. Minority participation in the Girl Scouts tripled.

In 1990, Hesselbein left the Girl Scouts after making it a first-class organization. She went on to become the founding president and CEO of the Peter F. Drucker Foundation for Nonprofit Management, and now serves as chairman of its board of governors. And in 1998, she was awarded the Presidential Medal of Freedom. President Clinton said of Hesselbein during the ceremony at the White House, "She has shared her remarkable recipe for inclusion and excellence with countless organizations whose bottom line is measured not in dollars, but in changed lives."[23] He couldn't have said it better!

WHY YOU SHOULD ENJOY THE RETURN OF BOTTOM-LINE THINKING

If you're accustomed to thinking of the bottom line only as it relates to financial matters, then you may be missing some things crucial to you and your organization. Instead, think of the bottom line as the end, the takeaway, the desired result. Every activity has its own unique bottom line. If you have a job, your work has a bottom line. If you serve in your church, your activity has a bottom line. So does your effort as a parent, or spouse, if you are one.

As you explore the concept of bottom-line thinking, recognize that it can help you in many ways:

1. Bottom-Line Thinking Provides Great Clarity

What's the difference between bowling and work? When bowling, it takes only three seconds to know how you've done! That's one reason people love sports so much. There's no waiting and no guessing about the outcome.

Bottom-line thinking makes it possible for you to measure outcomes more quickly and easily. It gives you a benchmark by which to measure activity. It can be used as a focused way of ensuring that all your little activities are purposeful and line up to achieve a larger goal.

2. Bottom-Line Thinking Helps You Assess Every Situation

When you know your bottom line, it becomes much easier to know how you're doing in any given area. When Frances Hesselbein began running the Girl Scouts, for example, she measured everything against the organization's goal of helping a girl reach her highest potential—from the organization's management structure (which she changed from a hierarchy to a hub) down to what badges the girls could earn. There's no better measurement tool than the bottom line.

3. Bottom-Line Thinking Helps You Make the Best Decisions

Decisions become much easier when you know your bottom line. When the Girl Scouts were struggling in the 1970s, outside organizations tried to convince its members to become women's rights activists or door-to-door canvassers. But under Hesselbein, it became easy for the Girl Scouts to say no. It knew its bottom line, and it wanted to pursue its goals with focus and fervency.

4. Bottom-Line Thinking Generates High Morale

When you know the bottom line and you go after it, you greatly increase your odds of winning. And nothing generates high morale like winning. How do you describe sports teams that win the championship, or company divisions that achieve their goals, or volunteers who achieve their mission? They're excited. Hitting the target feels exhilarating. And you can hit it only if you know what it is.

5. Bottom-Line Thinking Ensures Your Future

If you want to be successful tomorrow, you need to think bottom line today. That's what Frances Hesselbein did, and she turned the Girl Scouts around. Look at any successful, lasting company, and you'll find leaders who know their bottom line. They make their decisions, allocate their resources, hire their people, and structure their organization to achieve that bottom line.

HOW TO ENJOY THE RETURN OF BOTTOM-LINE THINKING

It isn't hard to see the value of the bottom line. Most people would agree that bottom-line thinking has a high return. But learning how to be a bottom-line thinker can be challenging.

1. Identify the Real Bottom Line

The process of bottom-line thinking begins with knowing what you're really going after. It can be as lofty as the big-picture vision, mission, or purpose of an organizaion. Or it can be as focused as what you want to accomplish on a particular project. What's important is that you be as specific as possible. If your goal is for something as vague as "success," you will have a painfully difficult time trying to harness bottom-line thinking to achieve it.

The first step is to set aside your "wants." Get to the results you're really looking for, the true essence of the goal. Set aside any emotions that may cloud your judgment and remove any politics that may influence your perception. What are you really trying to achieve? When you strip away all the things that don't really matter, what are you compelled to achieve? What must occur? What is acceptable? That is the real bottom line.

2. Make the Bottom Line the Point

Have you ever been in a conversation with someone whose intentions seem other than stated? Sometimes the situation reflects intentional deception. But it can also occur when the person doesn't know his own bottom line.

The same thing happens in companies. Sometimes, for example, an idealistically stated mission and the real bottom line don't jibe. Purpose and profits compete. Earlier, I quoted George W. Merck, who stated, "We try never to forget that medicine is for the people. It is not for the profits. The profits follow, and if we have remembered that, they have never failed to appear." He probably made that statement to remind those in his organization that profits *serve* purpose—they don't compete with it.

If making a profit were the real bottom line, and helping people merely provided the means for achieving it, then the company would suffer. Its attention would be divided, and it would neither help people as well as it could nor make as much profit as it desired.

3. Create a Strategic Plan to Achieve the Bottom Line

Bottom-line thinking achieves results. Therefore, it naturally follows that any plans that flow out of such thinking must tie directly to the bottom line—and there can be only one, not two or three. Once the bottom line has been determined, a strategy must be created to achieve it. In organizations, that often means identifying the core elements or functions that must operate properly to achieve the bottom line. This is the leader's responsibility.

The important thing is that when the bottom line of each activity is achieved, then THE bottom line is achieved. If the sum of the smaller goals doesn't add up to the real bottom line, then either your strategy is flawed or you've not identified your real bottom line.

4. Align Team Members with the Bottom Line

Once you have your strategy in place, make sure your people line up with your strategy. Ideally, all team members should know the big goal, as well as their individual role in achieving it. They need to know their personal bottom line and how that works to achieve the organization's bottom line.

5. Stick with One System and Monitor Results Continually

Dave Sutherland, a friend and former president of one of my companies, believes that some organizations get into trouble by trying to mix systems. He maintains that many kinds of systems can be successful, but mixing different systems or continually changing from one to another leads to failure. Dave says:

> Bottom-line thinking cannot be a one-time thing. It has to be built into the system of working and relating and achieving. You can't just tune into the desired result every now and then. Achieving with bottom-line thinking must be a way of life, or it will send conflicting messages. I am a bottom-line thinker. It is a part of my "system" for achievement. I practice it every day. No other measurements—no wasted efforts.

Dave used to call members of his field team every night to ask the bottom-line question they expect to hear. He continually kept his eye on the company's bottom line by monitoring it for every core area.

When it comes right down to it, regardless of your bottom line, you can improve it with good thinking. And bottom-line thinking has a great return because it helps to turn your ideas into results. Like no other kind of mental processing, it can help you to reap the full potential of your thinking and achieve whatever you desire.

Thinking Question

Am I staying focused on the bottom line so that I can gain the maximum return and reap the full potential of my thinking?

ONE FINAL THOUGHT

I trust you have enjoyed this book. As you move forward, I wish you success and suggest that you keep in mind . . .

1. **Everything begins with a thought.**
   "Life consists of what a man is thinking about all day."
   —RALPH WALDO EMERSON

2. **What we think determines who we are. Who we are determines what we do.**
   "The actions of men are the best interpreters of their thoughts."
   —JOHN LOCKE

3. **Our thoughts determine our destiny. Our destiny determines our legacy.**
   "You are today where your thoughts have brought you. You will be tomorrow where your thoughts take you."
   —JAMES ALLEN

4. People who go to the top think differently than others.

"Nothing limits achievement like small thinking; Nothing expands possibilities like unleashed thinking."

—WILLIAM ARTHUR WARD

5. We can change the way we think.

"Whatever things are true... noble... just... pure... lovely... are of good report. If there is any virtue and if there is anything praiseworthy; think on these things."   —PAUL THE APOSTLE

NOTES

1. James C. Collins and Jerry I. Porras, *Built to Last: Successful Habits of Visionary Companies* (New York: Harper Business, 1994), 213.

2. Joshua S. Rubinstein, David E. Meyer, and Jeffrey E. Evans, "Executive Control of Cognitive Processes in Task Switching," *Journal of Experimental Psychology*, quoted in *Leadership Strategies*, Volume 4, Number 12, December 2001.

3. Annette Moser-Wellman, *The Five Faces of Genius: The Skills to Master Ideas at Work* (New York: Viking, 2001), 6.

4. Annette Moser-Wellman, *The Five Faces of Genius: The Skills to Master Ideas at Work* (New York: Viking, 2001), 9.

5. Ernie J. Zelinski, *The Joy of Not Knowing It All: Profiting from Creativity at Work or Play* (Chicago: VIP Books, 1994), 7.

6. James Allen, *The Wisdom of James Allen* (San Diego: Laurel Creek Press, 1997).

7. Chris Palochko, "Security a Huge Issue at Super Bowl," sports.yahoo.com/nfl/news, February 2, 2002.

8. Bobb Biehl, *Masterplanning: A Complete Guide for Build-*

ing a Strategic Plan for Your Business, Church, or Organization (Nashville: Broadman and Holman, 1997), 10.

9. Janet Frankston, "Maxwell House Tie to Passover Spans Years," *The Atlanta Journal-Constitution,* March 27, 2002, F1.

10. Janet Frankston, "Maxwell House Tie to Passover Spans Years," *The Atlanta Journal-Constitution*, March 27, 2002, F10.

11. Chris Salewicz, *George Lucas* (New York: Thunders' Mouth Press, 1998), 113.

12. Eric Pooley, "Mayor of the World," *Time,* December 31, 2001, www.time.com.

13. Sally Kline (editor), *George Lucas: Interviews* (Jackson: University Press of Mississippi, 1999), 96.

14. Sally Kline (editor), *George Lucas: Interviews* (Jackson: University Press of Mississippi, 1999), 121.

15. "Leadership Lessons: An Interview with Don Soderquist," Willow Creek Association.

16. Mark Twain, *Following the Equator* (Hopewell, New Jersey: Ecco Press, 1996), 96.

17. Benno Muller-Hill, "Science, Truth, and Other Values," *Quarterly Review of Biology*, Volume 68, Number 3 (September 1993), 399–407.

18. Jeffrey J. Fox, *How to Become CEO* (New York: Hyperion, 1998), 115.

19. "Mectizan Program Removes Darkness from an Ancient Disease," *Corporate Philanthropy Report*, Merck, p. 11, www.merck.com, April 27, 2002.

20. Philippians 2:3–4 (NIV).

21. John A. Byrne, "Profiting from the Non-profits," *Business-Week*, March 26, 1990, 70.
22. John A. Byrne, "Profiting from the Non-profits," *Business-Week*, March 26, 1990, 72.
23. "Hesselbein Wins Presidential Medal of Freedom," www.drucker.org, December 19, 2001.

ABOUT THE AUTHOR

John C. Maxwell is a *New York Times*, *Wall Street Journal*, and *BusinessWeek* bestselling author, speaker, and coach who has sold more than 21 million books. He is the founder of EQUIP and the John Maxwell Company, organizations that have trained more than 5 million leaders in 173 countries. Each year he speaks to the leaders of diverse organizations, such as *Fortune* 100 companies, foreign governments, and National Football League, the U.S. Military Academy at West Point, and the United Nations. Read his blog at John MaxwellOnLeadership.com. Follow him at Twitter.com/ JohnCMaxwell.

Leadership expert and *BusinessWeek* and *New York Times* best-selling author John C. Maxwell shows you how to seize today.

MAKE TODAY COUNT

How can you know if you're making the most of today so you can have a better tomorrow? In this compact, hands-on guide, Maxwell offers daily disciplines that give maximum impact in minimal time. He shows how making twelve life-impacting decisions, then managing those decisions in just a few minutes a day, will empower you to clarify your own priorities and lead to a more successful and fulfilling life. Learn how to control your agenda, stretch your creativity and thinking, manage your money, improve and build relationships, nurture your personal growth, and much more. Start right now, and guarantee tomorrow's success by making today count.

Available now wherever books are sold.

Also available from

Hachette Audio

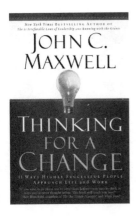

New York Times BESTSELLING AUTHOR OF
The 21 Irrefutable Laws of Leadership and *Running with the Giants*

JOHN C. MAXWELL

THINKING FOR A CHANGE

11 WAYS HIGHLY SUCCESSFUL PEOPLE
APPROACH LIFE and WORK

When your thinking is unlimited, so is your potential.

In *Thinking for a Change*, John C. Maxwell explores and identifies the specific skills you need to make your potential for success explode into results. This book won't tell you *what* to think, it tells you *how* to think. After all, success is as simple as changing your mind.

"If you want to go places you've never been before—you have to think in ways you've never thought before. This book will teach you how!"

—Ken Blanchard, coauthor of
The One Minute Manager® and *Whale Done!*

"In this important book, John Maxwell will teach you how to think in a way that will keep you ahead in these turbulent times and create exciting new opportunities and possibilities."

—Robert Kriegel, Ph.D., coauthor of
If It Ain't Broke . . . Break It!

Available now wherever books are sold.

New York Times best-selling author and expert on leadership John C. Maxwell shares the only rule that matters—in business and in life.

ETHICS 101

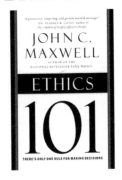

In the past few years, ethical lapses in corporate America have precipitated a need for change in business practices and business legislation. But is it always easy to see where the line is in life? What's the standard? And can it work in all situations? Maxwell thinks it can. His engaging book brilliantly demonstrates how people can live with integrity by using the Golden Rule as their standard—regardless of religion, culture, or circumstances.

"A persuasive, inspiring, and greatly needed message!"
—Dr. Stephen R. Covey, author of
The 7 Habits of Highly Effective People

Available now wherever books are sold.